LOGISTICS' CONTRIBUTIONS TO BETTER HEALTH IN DEVELOPING COUNTRIES

T0383762

Transport and Society

Series Editor: Margaret Grieco,
Professor of Transport and Society, Napier University, Scotland

This new series will focus on the impact of transport planning policy and implementation on the wider society and on the participation of the users. It will discuss issues such as gender and public transport, travel for the elderly and disabled, transport boycotts and the civil rights movement. Interdisciplinary in scope, it will link transport studies with sociology, social welfare, cultural studies and psychology.

Also in the series:

Integrated Futures and Transport Choices
Edited by Julian Hine and John Preston
ISBN 0 7546 1991 5

Urban Road Pricing: Public and Political Acceptability
Martin J. Whittles
ISBN 0 7546 3449 3

Transport Disadvantage and Social Exclusion
Julian Hine and Fiona Mitchell
ISBN 0 7546 1847 1

Re-Thinking Mobility
Vincent Kaufmann
ISBN 0 7546 1842 0

Shopping Choices with Public Transport Options
Muhammad Faishal Ibrahim and Peter J. McGoldrick
ISBN 0 7546 1810 2

Transport Lessons from the Fuel Tax Protests of 2000
Edited by Glenn Lyons and Kiron Chatterjee
ISBN 0 7546 1844 7

Logistics' Contributions to Better Health in Developing Countries

Programmes that Deliver

Edited by
PAT SHAWKEY
CAROLYN HART

Routledge
Taylor & Francis Group

LONDON AND NEW YORK

First published 2003 by Ashgate Publishing

Reissued 2018 by Routledge
2 Park Square, Milton Park, Abingdon, Oxon OX14 4RN
711 Third Avenue, New York, NY 10017, USA

Routledge is an imprint of the Taylor & Francis Group, an informa business

Publisher's Note
The publisher has gone to great lengths to ensure the quality of this reprint but points out that some imperfections in the original copies may be apparent.

Disclaimer
The publisher has made every effort to trace copyright holders and welcomes correspondence from those they have been unable to contact.

A Library of Congress record exists under LC control number: 2003052115

ISBN 13: 978-1-138-70903-4 (hbk)
ISBN 13: 978-1-138-70900-3 (pbk)
ISBN 13: 978-1-315-19841-5 (ebk)

Contents

List of Figures and Tables

Glossary

Acceptor A family planning user; also called a customer or client.

Adjustments Changes to inventory records to reflect losses or transfers of commodities, or to correct record keeping errors.

Bin card A stock-keeping record that records information about a single lot of a single product.

Bottom-up approach A strategy in which logistics system improvement begins at the field level, allowing field successes to generate policy-level interest and support (compare with *top-down approach*).

Burden of disease A methodology that combines health status, number of deaths, and impact of premature death and disability into a single unit of measurement.

Centralization The process of consolidating logistics management functions at higher levels of the organization.

Competency-based training Training designed to ensure that the knowledge and skills required to adequately carry out a job are developed under the guidance of an instructor.

Consumption rate The quantity of contraceptives given to users during a specified time period.

Consumption record A service record that records the quantity of contraceptives given to users (e.g., a daily activity register).

Contraceptive security When a reproductive health programme accurately estimates its commodity requirements, has (or coordinates) the financial and technical resources necessary to procure them, and ensures their reliable availability to end users, for the medium- to long-term future (at least 5–10 years).

Cost recovery A health reform initiative that introduces user fees to cover some of the recurrent health service costs.

Customer An individual who may want or require the goods and services provided by a specific programme. Used interchangeably with end user and client.

Customer service	In logistics, a set of values, attitudes, and procedures that make the customer the focal point for all supply chain operations.
Decentralization	A key strategy of the current health sector reform movement that pushes responsibility for health services management down to intermediate and lower levels.
Dejunking	Increasing the amount of usable storage space by clearing out obsolete, expired, and unusable items.
Demographic data	Contraceptive prevalence data, morbidity data, and other population statistics.
Dispensed to user data	Information on the quantity of products actually given to customers. Sometimes referred to as *dispensed* or *consumption data*. (See *issues data*.)
Distance education	Teaching skills or knowledge to trainees at a location away from the educational source, for example, using the Internet to present lessons.
Distribution	Logistics management function that includes inventory control, storage, and transporting products.
Distribution Resource Planning (DRP)	Software that can determine optimum delivery schedules and truck routings, based on projected stock levels at lower-level facilities.
Distribution system	Network of facilities where products are stored, coupled with transportation resources that move products through the network.
End user	Term used interchangeably with customer or client (for example, the family planning client).
First-to-expire, first-out (FEFO)	Inventory management system that ensures the products with the earliest expiry date are the first products issued. Moves older stock first to prevent expiries.
Forecasting	Logistics management function that estimates the quantity of each product that will be dispensed to customers (consumed) during a future period.
Full integration	A supply chain that handles all types of commodities and supplies in one system.

Graduation (also achieving self-reliance)	A stage when countries that traditionally received donated products and donor-funded logistics system support assume gradual or complete fiscal and managerial responsibility for contraceptive procurement and distribution.
Health information system (HIS)	A strategic management information system that gathers indicators of health service delivery system performance. May also be called health management information system (HMIS).
Intermediate customers	Service providers at service delivery points, and warehouses and stores, in the supply chain.
International competitive procurement	A purchasing method used to procure commodities through open competition among qualified suppliers, using transparent, accountable procedures.
Inventory management	Procedures that govern how supplies are received, stored, handled, and issued.
Issue voucher or requisition and issue voucher	A transaction record that lists the items and quantities of products issued to or requisitioned by a facility, along with quantities received.
Issues data	Information on the quantity of goods shipped from one level of a system to another (not quantities given to customers). (See *dispensed to user data*.)
Job aids	A job-based reference tool that helps staff perform a task.
Lead time	The interval between the date a product is ordered and the date it is received and available for use. Lead time varies depending on the system, speed of deliveries, availability and reliability of transport, and weather.
Logistics data (for forecasting)	The past quantities of each product dispensed to users or issued from level to level during a specific period.
Logistics management information system (LMIS)	A manual or computerized system that collects, processes, and reports logistics data. Provides managers with essential information for operational management of the logistics system. It should also collect and report accurate consumption data.

Logistics system	The total flow of products, from the acquisition of raw materials to the delivery of finished goods to users, including the related flow of information that controls and records the movement of those products.
Maximum/minimum (max/min)	An inventory control method that requires each facility to set maximum and minimum desired stock levels for each item to ensure that quantities fall within an established range.
Mission-critical	A task, item, or condition essential to the achievement of the chief function or responsibility of an organization or institution.
Modelling	When trainers or supervisors demonstrate a desired skill or behaviour that trainees later imitate.
Months of supply on hand	The quantity of stock on hand for each product expressed as the number of months that quantity should last, calculated by comparing quantities to average consumption.
On-the-job training	Pairing a trainee with an experienced colleague or supervisor to help the trainee acquire a set of specific skills.
Outsourcing	Hiring an outside vendor to provide services.
Overstock	A supply imbalance that occurs when stocks exceed the established maximum. May result in losses due to expiry.
Performance improvement	Improving individual and organizational effectiveness by identifying desired performance, recognizing the gap between desired and actual performance, and targeting interventions that focus on the skills, motivation, capacity, incentives, and environment needed for staff to perform their jobs well.
Pipeline	The entire chain of storage facilities and transportation links through which supplies move from manufacturer to consumer.
PipeLine	Requirements estimation software developed by FPLM/JSI.

Policy level Decision-makers who determine what services a health organization will provide, to whom, and with what funding.

Procurement Identification of suitable sources of supply and the acquisition of commodities according to a procurement plan, as economically as possible, within established quality standards.

Procurement planning Specifying the timing and quantities of products needed, based on the forecast, desired stock levels, and amounts already in stock or on order.

Product velocity The speed with which stock is used or issued. Products that move quickly are stored in the most accessible locations, while slower-moving items are stored at the back of the store or on the highest shelves.

Pull system Distribution system in which each lower-level facility pulls contraceptives through the supply chain by requisitioning (ordering) the required quantity at the time the contraceptives are needed. See *procurement*.

Push system Distribution system in which the higher-level facility decides what contraceptives to push through the supply chain, how many to push, and when and where to push them.

Requirements estimate An estimate developed to determine how much of any product must be procured, based on the forecast, desired stock levels, and amounts already in stock or on order.

Safety stock A buffer, cushion, or reserve stock kept on hand to protect against stockouts caused by delayed deliveries, increased demand, damage, or unexpected losses.

Service delivery point Any facility that serves clients directly; a place where customers receive supplies.

Service provider A provider of health services (doctor, nurse, pharmacist, volunteer health staff, and others).

Service statistics data   The number of new customers and revisits during a specific period. The number can be multiplied by the dispensing protocol (number of units supplied at a single visit) to yield data for commodity forecasts.

Shrinkage   Losses due to pilferage.

Stock-keeping records   Records used to track stock, including store ledgers, inventory control cards, and bin cards.

Stock on hand   The quantity of usable stock in inventory at a particular point in time. (Unusable items are *not* part of stock on hand.)

Stockout   Depleted supply of a given product or products; a zero stock balance.

Supply chain management   Coordinating different organizations and functions to source, produce, and deliver goods to customers.

Top-down approach   A strategy in which a programme begins by building a strong policy-level commitment to logistics improvement, followed by operational changes (compare with *bottom-up approach*).

'Top up' delivery system   A distribution system in which the delivery truck visits each facility on a regular schedule to deliver supplies needed to bring stock to its maximum level.

Transaction records   Forms used to track the movement of stocks from one facility to another, including issue vouchers, requisition and issue vouchers, and packing slips.

Understock   A supply imbalance that occurs when stocks fall below the established minimum. May result in unserved customers.

The Family Planning Logistics Management

The Family Planning Logistics Management (FPLM) project is funded by the Office of Population of the Bureau of Global Programs of the US Agency for International Development (USAID). The agency's Contraceptives and Logistics Management Division provides a centralized system for contraceptive procurement, maintains a database on commodity assistance, and supports a program for contraceptive logistics management.

Implemented by John Snow Inc. (contract no. CCP–C–00–95–00028–04), and subcontractors (The Futures Group International and the Program for Appropriate Technologies in Health [PATH]), the FPLM project works to ensure the continuous supply of high-quality health and family planning products in developing countries. FPLM also provides technical management and analysis of two USAID databases, the contraceptive procurement and shipping database (NEWVERN); and the Population, Health, and Nutrition Projects Database (PPD).

Acknowledgments

Logistics' Contributions to Better Health in Developing Countries: Programmes that Deliver is dedicated to friends and counterparts who have worked with Family Planning Logistics Management (FPLM) and John Snow Inc. (JSI) since 1986 – the tens of thousands of women and men in Ministries of Health and nongovernmental organizations around the world who work every day to supply their programs, and ultimately their customers, with essential products like contraceptives.

USAID contracts funded the technical assistance, in-country projects, and research that produced the lessons included in *Logistics' Contributions to Better Health in Developing Countries*. We are deeply grateful to the team of professionals in the Contraceptives and Logistics Management Division in the Office of Population of the USAID Global Bureau's Center for Population, Health, and Nutrition – especially Mark Rilling, John Crowley, and Naomi Blumberg – for their encouragement, advice, and commitment to improving public health through logistics.

Countless people helped write and rewrite this document – contributors, reviewers, writers, designers, editors, FPLM staff, consultants, counterparts, and clients. Sincere thanks go to JSI's Carolyn Hart, Richard C. Owens Jr, and Patrick Dougherty for their tireless efforts and their determination to leave this monograph as a legacy to all who work in logistics. Special thanks also go to Barbara Felling, Karen Ampeh, and Kieran McGregor and our colleagues at the Centers for Disease Control and Prevention for their significant contributions, particularly Susanna Binzen who collected and edited the many examples of program experience.

Field examples and data were generously contributed by Linda Allain, Claudia Allers, David Alt, Beatriz Ayala, Jim Bates, Barry Chovitz, Ibnou Diallo, Barbara Felling, Nurul Hossain, Shyam Lama, Ramona Lunt, Kieran McGregor, Paula Nersesian, Marilyn Noguera, Gideon Nzoka, David Papworth, Norbert Pehe, Walter Proper, Nora Quesada, Gary Steele, Daniel Thompson, Lois Todhunter, Bernardo Uribe, Frank White, Steve Wilbur, and John Wilson. Without their valuable assistance, this monograph would not have been written.

We acknowledge and sincerely thank the external reviewers who provided an essential perspective from the private sector, academia, nongovernmental organizations, and donor organizations:

Anthony Barone (logistics consultant, USA);
Andy Barraclough (development/logistics consultant, Thailand);
Andy Chesley (logistics engineer, USA);
Martin Christopher (professor of logistics, Cranfield University, UK);
Carl Hemmer (family planning consultant, USA);
Peggy Lee (professor of logistics, George Washington University);
Steve Perry (development/logistics consultant, USA);
Philip Price (professor of logistics, University of Alaska);
Timothy Rosche (development/logistics advisor, JSI);
Jagdish Upadhyay (logistics management advisor, UNFPA);
Alex Zinanga (family planning consultant, Zimbabwe).

The FPLM Communications Group edited, designed, and produced *Logistics' Contributions to Better Health in Developing Countries*. In particular, credit goes to Pat Shawkey, editor; Gus Osorio, graphic designer; Kristyn Kohl, photo editor; Jacalyn Ellis, reference editor; and Rachel Kaufman, editorial support.

Photographs on pp. 37 and 141 courtesy of Marcel Crozet/WHO. Photograph on p. 6 courtesy of Philip Lieberman of Brown University. Photograph on p. 55 courtesy of Lamia Jaroudi of JHU/CCP.

This document does not necessarily reflect the views or opinions of USAID. It may be reproduced if credit is given to FPLM/JSI and Ashgate Publishing Limited.

Abstract

Logistics, a mission-critical function in any health or family planning programme, ensures that essential products, necessary for any successful programme, are consistently available to customers. Policy makers and managers should understand that logistics or, more broadly, supply chain management makes critical contributions to programme impact, service quality, and cost-effectiveness. Modern supply chain management focuses more on people than on goods – the people who make the supply chain work and the customers who are served by the supply chain. The goal is to put products into the hands of customers.

In *Logistics' Contributions to Better Health in Developing Countries* examples from family planning and health logistics systems in Latin America, Africa, and Asia illustrate the major components of logistics operations: performance improvement, logistics management information systems, forecasting, procurement, and distribution (including inventory control, storage, and transport). A strategic process of diagnosing, planning, implementing, measuring, and monitoring can transform developing country family planning and health logistics systems from *as-is* to *could-be* operations. An improved logistics system, with strong leadership and a capable staff, provides more effective, efficient customer service. Improvements in public health supply chains can be measured by product availability at service delivery points and by cost ratios.

Global trends in health reform, donor policies, customer expectations, economics, and technology currently challenge all public health and family planning supply chains in developing countries. With adequate resources and policy-level support, *logistics helps programmes deliver*.

Executive Summary

The title of this book, *Logistics' Contribution to Better Health in Developing Countries: Programmes that Deliver*, has a double meaning. The first meaning is easily understood – you are going to read about logistics, the set of activities that move products through the supply chain to the ultimate customer. Clearly, logistics is a programme that delivers.

The second interpretation of the title is more significant – logistics activities contribute directly to family planning programmes' ability to deliver – to serve their customers and meet their objectives. For any health programme to deliver high-quality, comprehensive services, it must build and maintain a robust logistics system for essential products like contraceptives. This is the double meaning – when logistics delivers, programmes can deliver.

Logistics' Contribution to Better Health in Developing Countries was written and first published by the Family Planning Logistics Management (FPLM) project of John Snow Inc., a project funded since 1986 by the US Agency for International Development (USAID). In approximately 40 countries in Africa, Asia, Latin America, and the Caribbean, FPLM staff have been privileged to work with national family planning and health programmes and nongovernmental organizations interested in improving their supply chains. The contents of this book – the concepts, approaches, and lessons – are grounded in 15 years of practical collaboration.

Although it contains tips for managers, this publication is not a how-to guide for logistics practitioners. Instead, it was written to persuade the policy makers and senior managers of government ministries, service delivery organizations, and donor agencies to accept one simple truth: health and family planning programmes cannot succeed unless the supply chain delivers a reliable, continuous supply of contraceptives and essential products to customers. Our shorthand expression for this fact is, 'No product? No programme.' While four words cannot tell the whole story, we hope *Logistics' Contribution to Better Health in Developing Countries* does. Throughout the publication, in boxes, tables, graphs, and photos, real-life examples from the field illustrate points made in the text.

In chapters 1–3, you will read about our perspective, which includes a strategic framework for logistics. Chapter 1 explains how logistics contributes to the success of health and family planning programmes: their impact, quality, cost-effectiveness, accountability, and sustainability. Most health programmes consider logistics a low-profile component – largely forgotten unless something goes wrong, and then roundly blamed. Now is the time to recognize logistics' contribution as a mission-critical function of any health programme and to clarify the rationale for policy-level support.

Chapter 2 focuses on the policy maker's role in improving and supporting the supply chain. Logistics is often considered the most operational function, but its strategic importance is rarely understood. Based on successful experiences in both the commercial and public health sector in developing countries, chapter 2 argues for elevating the profile of the supply chain within the larger enterprise.

Chapter 3 presents a fresh perspective for developing country health and family planning logistics systems: the customer's perspective. During the past decade, a revolution has taken place in commercial sector logistics, firmly establishing a customer orientation throughout the supply chain. It is important to recognize that in any sector – retail, manufacturing, or public service – the logistics system exists to move products to end users – customers – not to store and properly count boxes or to load and unload trucks. To help health and family planning programmes function effectively, we advocate borrowing this mindset from the commercial sector. Chapter 3 suggests ways to persuade policy makers, senior managers, and logistics practitioners to adopt an attitude of customer service.

In chapter 4, you will explore the needs and motivations of the people and organizations that make logistics systems work, how organizations change, how effective performance improvement approaches work, and how strong leadership is critical for success. Chapter 4 also presents recommendations for helping staff learn to make supply chains work more effectively. When staff performance improves, organizational and logistics system performance improves, and contraceptives become increasingly available. Managers of successful supply chains make a significant investment in staff, and they see the results in a high standard of customer service.

In chapters 5, 6, and 7, you will read about the key components of a logistics system. You will find that these important topics are not treated in depth; rather, the chapters focus on essential information for a policy maker to expect from each component – to ensure appropriately designed, managed, and supported supply chains. Chapter 5 covers the fundamental importance of information in logistics – a customer-focused supply chain is driven by accurate, timely data. Chapter 6 discusses the related components of forecasting and procurement, two critical activities that ensure timely availability of products. Chapter 7 describes key elements of distribution and inventory control, including storage and transport.

In chapters 8 and 9 you will look into the future. Chapter 8 explains how systematic assessment can help transform a logistics system from its current state into a more efficient, effective, and resilient organization. And, finally, chapter 9 looks at the trends that affect and may transform family planning and public health supply chain management in developing countries – issues such as health sector reform, decentralization, cost recovery, the donor environment, and the role of the private sector.

Our message is: 'If you want programmes that deliver, invest in logistics.'

Whatever the future holds, we hope that you – the policy makers, programme managers, and donors – will find this book a valuable tool as you harness the power of logistics to design and implement *programmes that deliver*.

Chapter 1

Supply Chain Improvement: How it Benefits Family Planning Programmes

In Brief

Effective supply chains determine the success or failure of any public health programme – for example, without a reliable supply of contraceptives, a family planning programme cannot serve its customers. Both in business and in the public sector, decision makers increasingly direct their attention to improving supply chains, because logistics improvements bring important, quantifiable benefits. Supply chain improvements benefit public health programmes in three important ways:

- increased programme impact;
- enhanced quality of care;
- improved cost-effectiveness and efficiency.

The supply chain is a 'mission-critical' element of every health programme – something a programme requires to succeed or even to survive.

Examples in this and subsequent chapters are primarily from family planning, but they can apply to all health service delivery programmes, demonstrating logistics' contributions to the programme, the customer, and the bottom line.

Improving Family Planning: Programme Results

Public health programme results link directly to an effective, efficient supply chain. In family planning, for example, experiences from many countries have confirmed the relationship between improved contraceptive logistics and higher contraceptive prevalence rates, higher continuation rates, and lower total fertility rates.

Even in well-established, successful family planning programmes, contraceptive availability doesn't just happen – it must be supported by a

In the mid-1970s, the contraceptive prevalence rate in Bangladesh was approximately 7 per cent and the total fertility rate was 7 children per woman. During the intervening years, the contraceptive logistics system has made many improvements, providing more types of contraceptives and ensuring continuously available contraceptive supplies at all service delivery points. These and other programme initiatives helped increase the contraceptive prevalence rate to 51 per cent and decrease the total fertility rate to 3.4 children per woman.

The Kingdom of Jordan recently designed and installed a new contraceptive logistics system for family planning service providers. Representatives from every level of the main providers of family planning services – Ministry of Health (MOH) and the nongovernmental sector – cooperatively designed the system. With improvements in place, the occurrence of stockouts of any item fell from 85 to 29 per cent at the faculty level, and at the directorate level stockouts fell from 72 per cent to zero. With most facilities fully stocked in all contraceptive methods, contraceptive use rose dramatically, and the number of couple years of protection dispensed almost doubled in only two years.

carefully planned and managed logistics system. Conversely, family planning programmes with inadequate logistics support are plagued by irregular contraceptive availability. This can create a serious problem in rapidly expanding programmes when the supply chains do not keep pace with the growing number of customers. In the worst situation – when contraceptives are completely stocked out – services cannot be provided, regular customers go without contraceptives, and potential new customers are denied access to family planning. Customers quickly lose faith in the programme and stop asking for services.

Commercial retailers know that an available, affordable product attracts customers. The same is true for contraceptives: if the logistics system provides a reliable supply of contraceptives, more people are likely to try them. Readily available contraceptives encourage prospective family planning customers, and attracting new clients can raise contraceptive prevalence rates and lower fertility rates.

Customers feel more confident about the family planning programme when they have a constant supply of contraceptives – it motivates them to accept or continue a family planning method. A positive experience with family planning services also encourages clients to use other reproductive and child health services provided with family planning, contributing to improved overall health in a community.

In Jordan, a supply chain supervisor and health worker review clinic records.

Figures 1.1, 1.2, and 1.3 show the association between effective logistics and key programme indicators, such as contraceptive prevalence rate (CPR), couple years of protection (CYP), and total fertility rate (TFR). While other programme interventions and improvements took place during the same period, the results depict a remarkable parallel between the routine availability of supplies and overall programme performance.

Figure 1.1, from Kenya, displays the decrease in stockouts of the oral contraceptive Microgynon from 1989 through 1998 and the simultaneous increase in contraceptive prevalence for Microgynon, according to the preliminary results of the 1998 Kenya Demographic and Health Survey (DHS) (National Council for Population and Development 1998).

Figure 1.2, from Jordan, displays the dramatic increase in CYP from condoms and Microgynon from 1997 to 1998 (left side of graph). Note the abrupt decline in stockouts of those products during the same time (right side of graph) (Proper, Hart, and Mowaswas 1999).

Figure 1.3 displays the latest data from the 1999 Tanzania Reproductive and Child Health Survey; it indicates that both prevalence and product availability at service delivery points have continued to rise or improve (National Bureau of Statistics 2000).

In 1994, an external programme evaluation team reviewed data from matched pairs of facilities in two major surveys, the 1991 and 1994 Tanzania Demographic

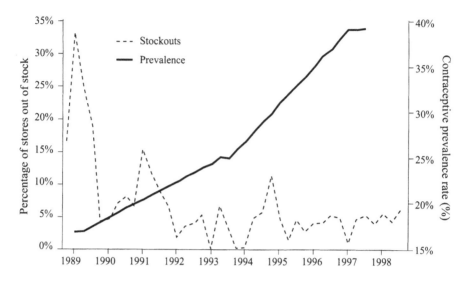

**Figure 1.1   Reduction in contraceptive stockouts in Kenya compared
to contraceptive prevalence rate**

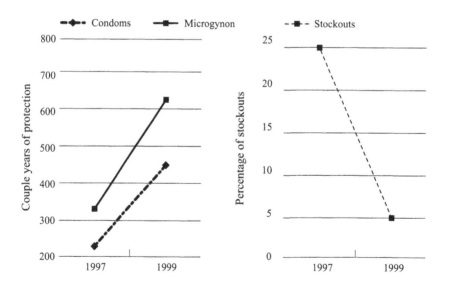

**Figure 1.2   Reduction in contraceptive stockouts in Jordan
compared to monthly couple years of protection**

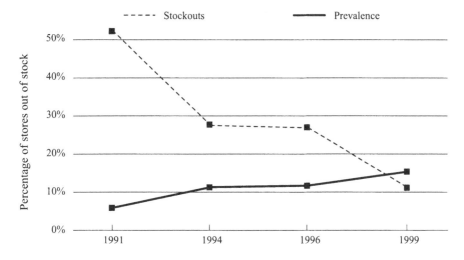

Figure 1.3   Reduction in contraceptive stockouts in Tanzania compared to contraceptive prevalence

and Health Surveys. They found a striking link between improved availability of supplies at service delivery points and CPR (Shutt et al., 1994; Ngallaba et al., 1993). During those years, Tanzania made an intensive effort to improve the supply chain. The availability of injectable contraceptives, for example, tripled at health centres (from 34 to 90 per cent of sites) and quadrupled at dispensaries (from 20 to 84 per cent of sites). Significant improvements were made in ensuring the availability of pills, intrauterine devices (IUD), and vaginal foaming tablets at all service delivery points, as well (Ngallaba et al., 1993). Nationwide, with more routine availability of products and a host of other programme improvements, modern method contraceptive prevalence more than doubled, from 7 per cent to 16 per cent, a remarkable programme achievement in just three years. Without a strengthened supply chain, this would have been impossible. Since 1994, the trends have continued to improve, and significant new efforts have been made to integrate family planning products into the medical stores department distribution system.

Improving Quality of Care

Quality of care in a family planning programme depends on the sustained availability of contraceptives.

This health officer in a rural service delivery point in Mustang, Nepal, supervises all contraceptives and drugs. He is the last link in the supply chain and, most important, he serves the ultimate customer.

An effective logistics system is a cornerstone of quality family planning programmes. Investments in the supply chain can directly improve quality of care, not only in the family planning programme, but throughout the health care system. The supply chain connects to quality of care in two ways:

1   quality of the products;
2   availability of products for customers and providers.

When people think of logistics and quality, they may first think of the quality of the products moving through the supply chain. A sound logistics system ensures the safety and efficacy of the products by routinely checking for quality throughout the procurement and distribution process. Clear and comprehensive product specifications are the first step in quality assurance, followed by routine sampling and testing during manufacture and upon receipt. Subsequently, the distribution system provides quality assurance by tracking expiration dates and ensuring good storage and handling practices.

The link between logistics and product quality is clear. The link between logistics and service quality may be less obvious, but it is equally important. Family planning organizations around the world use 'contraceptive availability' as one of the best overall quality of care indicators for their programmes. While there are many other components of high-quality service, quality of care in a family planning programme depends on the sustained availability of contraceptives (Bruce, 1990; Jain, 1989; Bulatao, 1995).

Well-supplied programmes can provide superior service, but poorly supplied programmes cannot. Likewise, well-supplied health workers can use their training and expertise fully, directly improving the quality of care for clients, but poorly supplied workers cannot provide quality care.

Customers are not the only ones to benefit from the consistent availability of contraceptives. An effective logistics system helps provide adequate, appropriate supplies to health providers, increasing their professional satisfaction, motivation, and morale. Motivated staff are more likely to deliver a higher quality of service. Conversely, it is demoralizing to family planning service providers when they receive an inadequate supply of contraceptives.

Reproductive health programmes work best when informed customers can choose their contraceptive method and know that method will be consistently available – not once, not sometimes, but always. An effective supply chain enables clients to select the contraceptive method they want. Especially in family planning, when customers voluntarily decide to use contraceptives, quality service depends on clients knowing that whatever method they choose, the contraceptive will be available.

Clinic staff welcome the prospect of reliable supplies. When the family planning programme in Jamaica pilot tested a 'top up' delivery system (a delivery truck visits every four months, and the delivery technician calculates the amount needed to top up supplies to their maximum level), clinic nurses in other parts of the country heard about the effective new system and began asking when their clinics would be added. Convinced that the new system would help them provide higher-quality service to their customers, the nurses were eager to learn how it worked and what role they would have in ensuring the reliable availability of essential products.

Improving Cost-effectiveness

An effective supply chain contributes to improved cost-effectiveness in all parts of a programme, and it can stretch limited resources. Strengthening and maintaining the logistics system is an investment that pays off in three ways. It:

1   reduces losses due to overstock, waste, expiry, damage, pilferage, and inefficiency;
2   protects other major programme investments;
2   maximizes the potential for cost recovery.

Every supply chain should ensure available products for customers at the lowest effective cost. Even in programmes that provide free or highly subsidized contraceptives, a cost is still associated with procuring and delivering the products to customers. Supply chain managers can use efficient

An MOH in Africa destroyed expired contraceptives worth tens of thousands of dollars. After implementing a nationwide inventory control system, no measurable expiries have been reported, and no contraceptives have been destroyed.

logistics operations to minimize this cost. For example, reducing the number of levels in a supply chain reduces overall logistics costs. A study in Bangladesh found that by reducing the distribution network from five levels to three, operating costs would be reduced by 66 per cent and transport costs by 29 per cent (FPLM 1997a). In addition, sound logistics systems have less waste, damage, and pilferage, preventing unnecessarily high programme costs.

By cutting losses and waste, an effective supply chain can significantly reduce a programme's overall costs. Contraceptive commodities may account for as much as 10–20 per cent of the total cost of a family planning programme. As a typical example, the budget for the Kenya family planning programme in 1993 was \$23.1 million; commodities valued at \$4.5 million made up approximately 19 per cent of the total cost (National Council for Population and Development 1995). If the logistics system works well, the budget for supplies and their distribution will go further.

> An effective supply chain enables clients to select the contraceptive method they want.

Another Kenyan example illustrates how improved logistics capabilities stretch commodity budgets. Kits for the diagnosis and treatment of sexually transmitted infections (STI) have been funded since 1995 by the British Department for International Development (DFID). Without accurate data on usage, and without a reliable distribution system, a \$600,000 supply of STI kits was projected to serve 143 sites for one year. With the design and implementation of a new tracking and distribution system, the same commodity budget for STI kits was used to supply more than 500 service sites for more than 29 months – vastly improving the cost-effectiveness of the effort and quintupling the expected impact (Regional Centre for Quality of Health Care, 1999a) (see Figure 1.4).

A study of the Central Medical Store in Malawi discovered a potential saving of \$350,000 if the store used better logistics management to correct overstocking (Ayala, 1999). Two years of focused hard work by the Malawi Ministry of Health created a reliable, well-functioning supply chain for contraceptives. The new system requires less buffer stock, further reducing overall programme costs.

Strengthening the supply chain protects more than just the investment in commodities. Staff salaries may account for as much as 50–70 per cent of family planning programme costs. A well-supplied staff can use their training and expertise fully – without supplies, however, these expensive

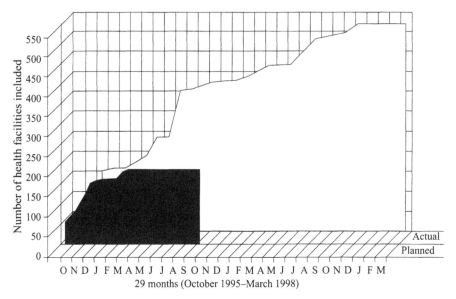

Figure 1.4   Improvement of actual over planned distribution of sexually transmitted infection kits in Kenya

human resources are wasted. Similarly, large investments in recruitment and training, facilities, information, education, and community mobilization are wasted when contraceptives are unavailable. Without a product, there is no programme.

It is a well-known adage in business that you cannot sell what you do not have, and a missed sale is lost revenue. The same is true for public health and family planning programmes. As part of their cost recovery, co-payment, privatization, or social marketing efforts, many health and family planning programmes offer products for sale. A lost sale of contraceptives, a missed or underserved customer, creates an underachieving programme.

No Product? No Programme

Practical Tips for Programme Managers: How to Highlight the Benefits of Logistics

Programme managers and logistics system managers can take the following steps to help policy makers understand the contributions sound logistics can make to overall programme effectiveness:

- gather good product availability, service utilization, and programme cost data;
- compile the information accurately, analyse it creatively, and use it to explain to policy makers the linkages between logistics and programme impact, customer service, and cost-effectiveness.
- present the data in an easy-to-understand format (eye-catching graphs and charts, and carefully selected statistics);
- understand and respond to the specific concerns of specific policy makers (for example, it is doubtful that a minister of finance will be interested in programme impact statistics, but he *will* be interested in numbers that show cost-effectiveness; a permanent secretary of health may be most interested in numbers of customers served well);
- throughout the organization, reinforce the message that the supply chain makes a crucial contribution to the success of the overall programme. Logistics is a mission-critical function.

Bringing it Together: Policy Makers' Perspective on the Benefits of Logistics Improvements

Everyone cares deeply about at least one of logistics' three contributions: impact, quality, or cost-effectiveness. At the policy level, usually all three are key motivations. Policy makers responsible for public health and family planning programmes care about their nation's health. They have dedicated their professional lives to building programmes that deliver critical public health services, such as family planning. To do this, they must care about programme impact. Many decision makers in the health sector are also trained as clinicians; others have been clients in the health care system. Either way, they understand the importance of quality of care. As public officials and senior bureaucrats, public health decision makers also have financial and fiduciary responsibility for public funds, and they are accountable to their governments for sound management. Clearly, their positions require them to focus on cost-effectiveness.

As policy makers learn how sound logistics helps programmes achieve results, they will support logistics as one of their most effective tools in raising the impact, improving the quality, and increasing the efficiency of their programmes.

Chapter 2

Policy Environment: Winning and Maintaining Policy Support for Supply Chain Improvements

In Brief

Only with political support can a programme ensure a reliable supply of contraceptives and other health commodities while sustaining its supply chain. The policy level (the decision makers who determine what services a health organization will provide, to whom, and with what funding) needs to support logistics as a 'mission-critical' function. To support programmes, the policy level needs to understand and appreciate what logistics is and how it works. Policy makers need to know what results to expect and at what cost.

The visibility of the logistics function at the policy level cannot be assumed or taken for granted. First, awareness, then support, must be established and maintained as policy makers and policies change, as family planning and health programmes mature, and as customers become more demanding.

With this publication, we provide information that will help establish a receptive policy environment for supply chain logistics within MOHs, local nongovernmental organizations (NGO), and international agencies. This chapter highlights the role of policy makers in creating effective, modern, customer-oriented logistics systems.

Creating a Policy Framework for Supply Chain Improvement

Creating a successful supply chain requires top-level support. This is true in the commercial sector, where senior executives understand what the supply chain does for their business; it is true in the public sector, where policy makers and senior public officials create and guide programmes providing needed services and products.

This chapter explains how to create a policy framework for supply chain improvement – from gaining policy makers' support to changing the organization. We provide guidelines for establishing and maintaining policy-level support, and we discuss how different approaches to supply chain improvement involve the policy level.

Borrowing language from the commercial sector, we use some terminology that may be new to the public health policy maker. Throughout this publication, we refer to customers and customer service; logistics, logistics systems, and supply chain management; and pipeline and supply chain. You should understand the meaning of these terms in the context of this publication.

Senior executives need to understand how the supply chain helps fulfil their organization's mission.

Customers, current and potential, are individuals who may desire or require the goods and services provided by a specific programme. For health and family planning programmes, customers' characteristics include age, sex, literacy, marital status, number of pregnancies, presence of sexually transmitted diseases, preference for spacing or limiting births, preference for certain contraceptive methods, and proximity to a health facility, among others. These individuals are often called 'acceptors' or 'clients'. We prefer the term 'customer' to indicate a new, more active, respectful, and accountable orientation.

Customer service in logistics is a set of values, attitudes, and procedures that make the customer the focal point for all supply chain operations. This is likely to be a new perspective for most managers working in logistics. Chapter 3 explores the customer focus in detail. A customer orientation in logistics means the supply chain structure and procedures work together to deliver products efficiently to the end user. This new focus may require changes in the attitudes and behaviour of staff throughout the supply chain – from the policy-level decision maker to the direct service provider, and every manager and storekeeper in between.

Logistics, *logistics system*, and *supply chain management* are terms for the set of activities that control how materials and products move, from the initial source to the end user. In the broadest definition, the logistics system includes the total flow of products, from the acquisition of raw materials to the delivery of finished goods to users, as well as the related flow of information that both controls and records the movement of those materials. However, in a narrower definition, logistics comprises the supply activities of just one organization. Supply chain management, on the other hand, includes the many different organizations that must be orchestrated to source, produce, and deliver goods to customers.

The *pipeline* includes the entire chain of storage facilities and transportation links that move supplies from the manufacturer to the consumer, including port facilities, central warehouses, regional warehouses, district and subdistrict stores, service delivery points, and transport vehicles. Not every logistics system will have all levels (leaner systems have fewer levels), but every logistics system has a pipeline of linked entities that move products to users.

Establishing executive or policy-level support is a vital task for anyone trying to improve the availability of contraceptives and essential health supplies. Establishing the required support among top executives is not done just once – but over and over again. In a cyclical way, customer service expectations, policy leadership and support, logistics improvements, and customer service improvements all reinforce each other.

The cycle can begin at any juncture (see Figure 2.1):

- start the cycle with logistics improvements – which produce improvements in customer service, which raise customer expectations, which influence new policies and commitments to the public;
- start with better customer service or heightened customers' expectations – which create awareness, stimulate leadership, and generate support at the policy level for further logistics improvements;

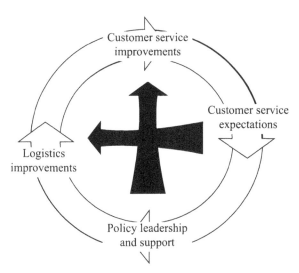

Figure 2.1   Cycle for a customer-driven supply chain

- or, start with policy leadership – which enhances the supply chain, which delivers improved customer service, which raises customers' expectations, which goes around again to influence the policy level to further support logistics system improvements.

There are other relationships as well, designated by the gray arrows, but Figure 2.1 illustrates the process of continuous improvement that can result when the policy level, supply chain, and customers interact.

When policy makers understand the contributions the logistics system makes to programme impact, quality of care, and cost-effectiveness (discussed in Chapter 1), they can become important advocates for ensuring continued logistics support.

There are two aspects to executive or policy-level support for a customer-driven supply chain:

1   a firm commitment to make logistics improvements that focus on the unfailingly reliable availability of all products at all service sites and outlets;
2   support for management development in general. Developing the customer focus required to operate a successful supply chain is likely to require broader changes in the way public health service organizations are structured and managed.

Win Policy Makers' Support

Winning policy makers' support for logistics improvements is the first step. Policy makers need to:

- *understand* the vital role played by logistics in successful family planning and health programmes.
- *value* the tangible benefits of effective supply chain management to the programme and the customer.
- *ensure* that all customers are reliably supplied with their contraceptives of choice and other health products.

As an example, Dr Colonel Adama Ndoye, Director of the National Family Planning Programme of Senegal, a champion of logistics, fights to bring logistics to the forefront. Colonel Ndoye became interested in logistics when he discovered that many regions in Senegal were stocked out of contraceptive supplies. From this experience, he realized that the logistics system is the *'nerf de la guerre* [sinew or strength] of any family planning programme'. As Colonel Ndoye says, 'without the regular availability of the right contraceptives, one cannot begin to talk about family planning nor about reproductive health programmes'.

Clearly, but perhaps unexpected, there are logistics similarities in principle and practice among the global retail explosion of the 1980s and 1990s, the traditional mission of logistics in the military, and a public health programme's customer-focused supply chain. As the leaders at the policy level of their organizations – ministers and secretaries of health, chief executive officers and chairmen of the board, generals and commanding officers – they have much in common. Listen to the voices from the private sector and the military and note how relevant their guiding principles are to the public health supply chain.

Change the Organization

Creating change to improve logistics within a bureaucratic organization requires key ingredients. Three leaders at a Council of Logistics Management meeting in 1999 suggested strategies to move bureaucratic, public sector organizations toward logistics excellence (Glisson, Handy, and McCissock, 1999).

- *Exhibit leadership.* Senior leader commitment to change is the key. It must be total, long-term commitment.
- *Clarify the mission.* Start the discussion at the point of purpose – the mission of the organization. When supply chain workers focus on the end user of the supplies delivered by the logistics system, they are more effective.
- *Involve people.* Successful implementation of a supply chain requires workers to be integrated at all levels: policy, management, and operations.
- *Use information.* Visualize the future, especially the role of information. Understand where you are going and use information to guide you. The ultimate success of the supply chain depends upon information.
- *Challenge the status quo.* One role of the policy level is to detect the need for change, to witness personally the requirement to change, and to say, 'I don't know what the solution is, but the situation must change'. The role of a policy leader is to challenge the status quo and constantly redefine success.

Former military logistics commander Lieutenant General Gus Pagonis, now working in the private sector as executive vice president at Sears, Roebuck and Company, offers this advice to improve the supply chain (Pagonis, 1992):

- *Keep it simple.* Develop and widely disseminate an organizing vision of the logistics operation. Use every single tool at your disposal to disseminate and reinforce your plans and visions. Simplify your message, and then communicate that message relentlessly.
- *Emphasize training.* It is not enough to disseminate the vision and the plan; leadership must ensure that the work force has the necessary skills to act on the vision.
- *Go for flexibility.* It's unfair to ask the work force to be flexible without demanding the same from the organization. The leader must ensure that organizational rules and structures don't get in the way of performance.
- *Centralize planning; decentralize execution.* Centralized planning prevents suboptimization among functional departments – in the logistics field and elsewhere. It creates the screen through which ideas, good and bad, can be filtered. Equally important is decentralized execution. People need to have a vision and a plan, be trained, and then turned loose.
- *Communicate!* What makes the contradictory tugs between centralization and decentralization work? The answer is communication. Disagreements should be treasured (and resolved).
- *Be visible. Be real.* The challenge of the leader is to be real to the organization. Being visible and accessible is a great way to get there. Get out, listen, talk, and be visible.

A final voice from the private sector, Mary Lou Quinto, Director of Logistics International, SmithKline Beecham plc, offers advice after undertaking a major reorganization of her company's supply chain (Murray and Quinto, 1999): 'I wouldn't have touched a project of this type and scale without sponsorship from the very top'.

In developing countries' family planning programmes, one way to convince policy makers of the importance of an effective logistics system is to start small, usually with a pilot project or limited system, and demonstrate success. In the early 1990s, in the Philippines, the Department of Health implemented a new Contraceptive Distribution and Logistics management information system (CDLMIS). After implementation, the constant complaints about the lack of contraceptive supplies dropped dramatically. Aware of the widespread unavailability of essential child survival drugs in the service outlets, the Department of Health staff working in the child survival programme noted this

Department of Health logistics staff in the Philippines deliver contraceptives and child survival supplies to the health facility.

success. In a pilot test, five essential drugs were added to the CDLMIS system. When the critical health products were effectively distributed and managed without affecting the availability of contraceptives, policy makers were convinced that a similar system was needed for essential drugs. Nationwide rollout of an essential drugs distribution system has been complicated by governmental devolution, but with a lasting commitment at the policy level to product availability, such complications can be overcome, and a reliable supply chain can be developed.

Establish the Policy Makers' Role

What is the role of the policy maker working in public health service delivery in a developing country? What does the policy maker do? What should the policy maker do?

• *Create and communicate the vision for the entire organization.* What is the vision for your organization? Is it a commitment to the public? Is your slogan, 'We provide a basic package of health services to all people'? Perhaps it is, 'Our programmes deliver'. Whatever it is, clarify it, simplify it, and communicate it relentlessly so that everyone in the organization understands, including those working on the supply chain.

- *Identify and communicate the mission of logistics and role of the supply chain in fulfilling that vision.* At Wal-Mart, with its 'lowest possible price' vision, the need for efficiency, speed, and flexibility in the supply chain is obvious now, but when Wal-Mart started it was a revolutionary business decision to exploit logistics that way. What is the best way to identify and communicate the role of logistics in your organization? Is it, 'No one should ever leave a clinic empty-handed'? Perhaps, it is, 'Good logistics delivers better health'.

- *Communicate and use information.* Logistics information has been described as the lubricant that keeps the organizational machine running. It is the policy makers' role to insist that their managers create an organization that shares and uses information.

- *Delegate authority.* After policy makers have promised to support supply chain logistics, the key policy support needed is delegation of authority. This will enable operations-level staff to implement logistics improvements.

- *Allocate resources.* The policy level controls the resource allocation process. Be sure that the supply chain operation has adequate resources to function properly – an appropriate number of effective managers and trained staff; adequate quantities of up-to-date equipment and facilities; and clear, well-documented policies and procedures.

- *Stay in touch.* The overall effectiveness of the health service organization will improve if policy makers know how the logistics system is functioning. Managers and their staff feel gratified and empowered when the policy level shows interest in their work. Asking policy makers to stay in touch with the supply chain does not mean micromanagement, but it does mean keeping logistics and supply issues on the policy agenda, and asking for and using current logistics information for programme decision making.

With policy support for contraceptive logistics, family planning programmes thrive. In Mexico, logistics is recognized as a key component of the reproductive health programme of the Mexican Social Security Institute (IMSS). Top-level officials, aware of the benefits, have an impressive record of providing financial and political support to the IMSS supply chain, whenever needed.

Sam Walton and the Wal-Mart retail chain revolutionized the role of logistics. Walton explains the Wal-Mart philosophy (Walton, 1992):

'Here's the point. The bigger Wal-Mart gets, the more essential it is that we think small ...

If we ever forget that looking a customer in the eye, greeting him or her, and asking politely if we can be of help is just as important in every Wal-Mart store today as it was in [the first little store], then we just ought to go into a different business because we'll never survive in this one.'

Wal-Mart's supply chain supports that vision by 'thinking small':
1 Serve one store at a time. The objective of the supply chain – serving customers – is achieved store by store, department by department, customer by customer.
2 Communicate, communicate, communicate. Keep a constant flow of communication through meetings, phone calls, information system reports, pep talks, and seminars.
3 Keep your ear to the ground. Managers need to get out of their offices and into their facilities for a real 'hands-on, get-down-in-the-store' perspective.
4 Push responsibility – and authority – down. Allow operations-level staff to be 'managers of their own businesses', and to identify and implement improvements.
5 Force ideas to bubble up. Encourage managers to propose ideas for new ways to work.
6 Stay lean, fight bureaucracy. As organizations grow, duplication can build up. 'If you're not serving the customer, or serving the folks who do, we don't need you.'

In the Chilean national budget, money is allocated specifically for contraceptives. The MOH is so convinced of the importance of a good logistics system to protect the investment in commodities that it is spending its own money to develop software to track inventory movement and consumption.

Guidelines for Establishing and Maintaining Policy Support

In many countries, logistics has not traditionally enjoyed strong policy-level support (Dadzie, 1998; Stock, 1990). Therefore, building a receptive policy environment may be a long-term process requiring diligence, patience,

Four workers in Senegal load a large open truck while their supervisor watches.

and hard work for mid- to senior-level managers. The following practical guidelines, based on experiences in many countries, may help operational staff build policy support for the supply chain.

*   *Hold discussions and meetings with key policy makers and programme officers.* Relaxed, informal, face-to-face discussions about supply chain management are a simple, effective way to build a favourable policy environment for supply chain improvements. Managers should plan and schedule discussions and meetings carefully to include all policy framework stakeholders. Don't forget to include executives from the financial, service delivery, promotional, and statistical sections of the organization. They all need to understand and support the supply chain.
*   *Attend and participate in conferences, workshops, and other formal meetings.* Take advantage of opportunities to increase the visibility of logistics; highlight its impact on family planning and health programme results and on customer satisfaction. Make sure the presentations address the concerns of the policy level: impact, quality, and cost.

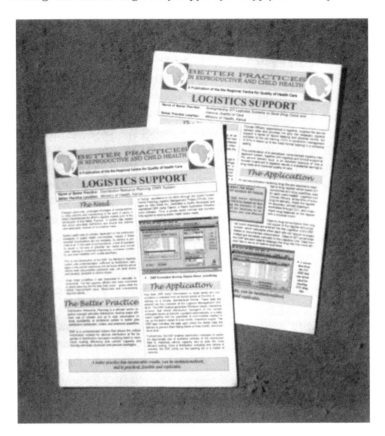

In Kenya, a Better Practices flyer provides information about supply chain improvements for policy makers, donors, and the public.

- *Conduct logistics seminars and workshops for policy makers and programme officers.* Periodic seminars and workshops for policy makers and programme managers on supply chain management and how to make contraceptives available to customers are excellent ways to maintain a receptive policy environment for supply chain logistics.
- *Identify a 'logistics champion' within the organization's hierarchy.* Whether an MOH or NGO, every organization has individuals who make things happen. From this group, identify someone with decision-making authority (or at least an influence on decision making) to lobby at the policy level for improved supply chain management. The logistics champion can popularize the numerous programme benefits of improved logistics and the benefit of using a customer service model to help focus logistics

improvements. The champion must know how to get the attention of policy makers and how to ensure policy support for a dependable contraceptive supply for all customers.

- *Identify potential supporters outside the parent organization.* Many organizations – international donor agencies, government ministries or programmes, and nongovernmental organizations – may want to guarantee a reliable supply of contraceptives for customers. Seek out potential allies and make them part of the policy framework for your supply chain. Some organizations may provide financial support for logistics improvements, while others may apply gentle pressure at the policy level to move forward with proposed supply chain improvements.

- *Deliver the goods.* Success in delivering the goods – providing customers with a reliable supply of contraceptives – will enhance the policy environment for supply chain logistics by protecting senior decision makers from public and political criticism for ineffective programmes. Use regular reports from the logistics management information system to bring logistics successes to policy makers' attention.

- *Highlight supply chain achievements in organizational reports and publications.* Widely disseminate supply chain improvements and the benefits to customers. Even if busy policy makers do not read an entire newsletter or annual report, published results will raise the profile of logistics and help maintain policy-level awareness of supply chain management.

- *Establish a policy-level logistics committee.* Form a special logistics committee of key decision makers and donors to build and maintain a strong policy framework for supply chain management. The committee can be a focal point for policy decisions needed to enhance the supply chain; it should keep logistics squarely in the strategic, not just operational, side of the organization.

  - *Be systematic and thorough in building a strong policy framework for logistics.* Avoid these common pitfalls:
  - assuming that a supportive policy environment will happen automatically without a systematic effort;
  - thinking that a supportive policy framework can be created in an ad hoc way during normal interaction with policy makers;
  - resting when you think you have secured adequate policy-level support.

  All three assumptions are wrong. Serious time and attention must be devoted to establishing and maintaining political support for logistics improvements.

- Develop and adhere to a plan with measurable objectives. For example, to improve the customer focus of the supply chain and the overall performance of the programme, you might set objectives like:
  - conduct a half-day seminar on supply chain logistics to emphasize programme benefits and the need for a customer orientation. At least 90 per cent of the department heads, regional health officers, and district health officers responsible for family planning will have participated by June 2001;
  - reduce stockouts of any products, at any time, to less than 5 per cent at all service delivery points and less than 10 per cent at all district stores. These reductions will be complete by December 2001. (Note that the targets indicate a customer-oriented supply chain – they would rather suffer stockouts at a higher level than at the service site!)

**Malawi used a bottom-up approach to improve its supply chain.
They reduced stockouts and made contraceptives more available to
customers, like these women at a local health clinic.**

Using Bottom-up and Top-down Approaches for Supply Chain Improvement

Family planning programmes have successfully used both bottom-up and top-down approaches to improve their logistics systems. A bottom-up approach to logistics improvement means beginning at the field level and allowing field successes to generate policy-level interest and support. During 1998, Malawi used a bottom-up approach by first establishing a field-level distribution and logistics information system that reduced stockouts and made contraceptives more available to customers. The favourable outcome attracted the attention of policy makers, and a receptive policy environment for supply chain improvements developed from these first field-level successes. Malawi's new policy environment enabled it to tackle a broad range of supply chain improvements, including the eventual merger of contraceptives and pharmaceuticals into an integrated supply system. Figure 2.2 shows the dramatic decrease in stockouts from 1998 to 1999.

In Figure 2.2, the left side of the graph shows the percentage of service delivery points that experienced any stockout of any product. The right side of the graph shows the stockout percentages for two sample products: progestin-only pills (POP) and condoms.

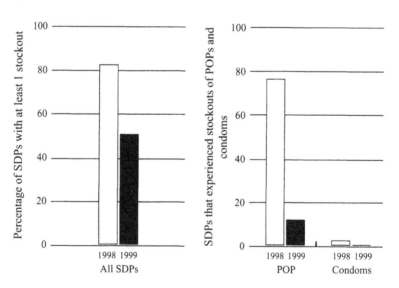

Figure 2.2   Contraceptive stockouts at service delivery points in Malawi between 1998 and 1999

A top-down approach means first building a strong policy-level commitment to logistics improvement, then, with the full backing of well-informed policy makers, enhancing supply chain operations within this policy environment. Beginning in 1997, Jordan successfully combined this top-down approach with strong field-level interventions. With high-level policy support, Jordan's Ministry of Health implemented a new, highly effective contraceptive logistics system that included all the major providers of family planning services in the country.

Representatives from every level in the MOH in Jordan participated in a workshop to design the new logistics management information system. Recommendations for the final system were presented formally and informally to ministry policy makers. The policy makers' approval of the new system resulted in nationwide training and detailed manuals for each level. Within two years, from 1997 to 1999, all service delivery and directorate-level supervisory staff had been trained, and the new information system was collecting essential logistics data and regularly producing accurate, timely reports for all levels of the system. With the policy makers' support, these dramatic improvements were made in a relatively short time.

Figure 2.3 shows the dramatic decrease in stockouts, based on 100 per cent reporting from all the MOH health centres and more than 98 per cent reporting from all participating service delivery points in the country.

A service delivery programme or organization can select either strategy – bottom-up or top-down – or a combination of the two. A bottom-up approach encourages and enables a cumulative field success to build the same strong framework, while a top-down approach requires the programme to build a strong policy framework for contraceptive and drug logistics first. Regardless of the approach used to ensure the long-term sustainability of supply operations, the policy level eventually must welcome and support logistics. They must respect the value of the supply chain in strengthening the family planning or health programme by providing customers with reliable, safe, effective supplies.

Programmes that deliver require good supply chains!

Bringing it Together: What the Supply Chain Needs from the Policy Level

The supply chain first needs to be recognized by the policy level. Programme leaders need to recognize, promote, and sustain the role of logistics in any

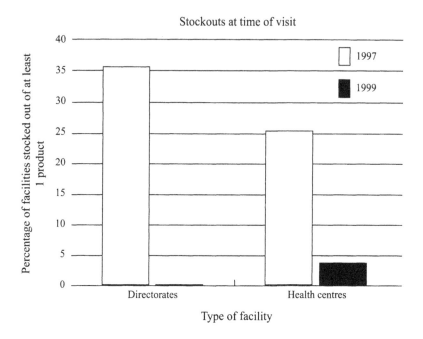

Figure 2.3   Contraceptive stockouts at health centres and directorates in Jordan between 1997 and 1999

public health programme. To do this, managers must promote to policy makers the important role of logistics in their health programmes (see below).

Second, policy makers need to include, not isolate, logistics system managers. Supply considerations are critical to many broad, strategic, policy-level issues, such as decentralization, cost-recovery, and programme expansion – yet senior logisticians are often left out of the discussions. This is where the lessons from the private sector are relevant: the logistics function is fully integrated into successful businesses; it often drives and sustains the entire enterprise.

Third, and most obvious, the supply chain needs to be adequately resourced with top-quality leadership, up-to-date equipment and facilities, and trained personnel. Correctly resourced, the logistics system returns far more to the organization than it costs.

Practical Tips for Logistics Managers

- Take time away from the warehouse and make yourself known to policy makers. Be confident and assertive.
- Ask to attend relevant policy meetings. Determine how the decisions being made by policy makers can or do affect your particular activities and responsibilities.
- Determine what you want from policy makers, and get on their agenda.
- Look for new ways to solve old problems. Focus on meeting customers' needs and improving logistics procedures.
- Identify and communicate a clear, concise vision for the logistics system, consistent with the overall organization's mission.
- Be a leader and seek out other leaders in the larger organization to build support for a stronger customer orientation throughout the organization.
- Communicate continually with policy makers and with your staff.
- Make sure your staff have the training they need to do their jobs.
- Be persistent.

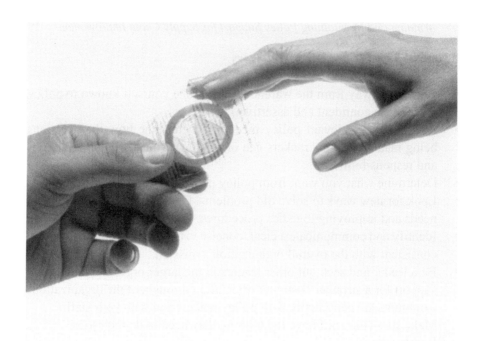

Chapter 3

The Customer: Ultimate Beneficiary of Supply Chain Management

In Brief

From acquiring raw materials to delivering finished products to end users, logistics operations include all the activities along the logistics cycle, from 'the suppliers' supplier to the customer's customer'. This is the supply chain. In a well-functioning supply chain, at every link, each unit should treat the next unit as a customer, always focusing on service to the ultimate customer, the end user. In a health or family planning programme, the end user – for example, the family planning client – is the final beneficiary of supply chain management.

Policy makers, programme managers, and supply chain staff should know their customers and what they want. They should focus all logistics operations on satisfying their customers' needs.

Serving the Customer: A Fresh Approach to Ensuring Contraceptive Availability

In the private commercial sector, the philosophy of service to the customer revolutionized supply chain management. A strong customer focus is the hallmark of progressive, successful logistics operations. The same philosophy can and should apply in public sector health and family planning programmes. By putting customers first, programmes in many countries are already improving customer service.

Customer service in logistics means focusing on the customer, replacing the traditional focus on goods. When the customer is the focus of logistics improvements, programme managers can streamline and improve supply chain management to provide their ultimate customers with a reliable supply of contraceptives and other essential health products. Figure 3.1 depicts the many levels of the in-country pipeline, all of which exist to move products to the end users.

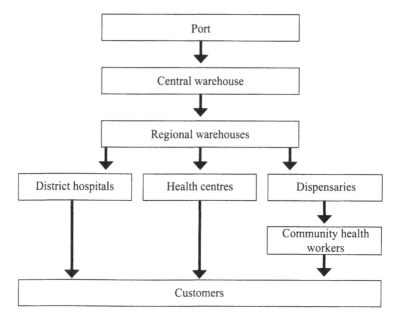

Figure 3.1   Basic in-country supply pipeline

Customers of public health and family planning programmes depend on the logistics system for a continuous supply of contraceptive products. When the supply chain fails, customers cannot obtain the contraceptives or other supplies they need and want. If this happens often enough, the programme loses credibility and, eventually, may fail.

Giving Family Planning Customers What They Want

Contraceptive supply chain managers have one primary customer – the family planning client. Policy makers can judge proposed logistics improvements or other programme changes by asking: how will this benefit the family planning customers?

Family planning customers need:

- a dependable supply of contraceptives of their choice;
- quality contraceptives in good condition and ready to use;
- contraceptives available when and where they want them;
- contraceptives available at an affordable cost.

Notice how the needs of family planning customers directly relate to the widely known 'six rights' of the logistics system.

Logistics fulfils the six rights by delivering:

1   the right product;
2   in the right quantity;
3   in the right condition;
4   to the right place;
5   at the right time;
6   for the right cost.

Staff of well-functioning supply chains anticipate and satisfy their customers' contraceptive needs. Some family planning organizations, however, ignore customer service when they plan their contraceptive supply chains, resulting in unserved acceptors, diminished programme results, and waste.

A successful programme does more than make contraceptives available in certain locations; the locations must be convenient, and the availability of essential health products must be widely known. For example, a group of Albanian women participating in a study thought that contraceptives were only available in pharmacies and were too expensive for them to buy. The women did not know that contraceptives were available free of charge in the public sector clinics and had been for some time. For maximum effectiveness, the supply chain must be integrated with other aspects of the programme – including promotion and service delivery.

Serving Intermediate Customers in the Supply Chain

> The logistics system exists to supply quality products to every customer.

Supply chain managers, in addition to their ultimate customers, also have important intermediate customers, each with special needs and expectations:

Service providers (doctors, nurses, pharmacists, dispensers, community-based distributors, volunteer health workers, and others) are the final link in the long supply chain that stretches from contraceptive manufacturers to family planning customers. Because they directly connect logistics operations to the ultimate customer, service providers at service delivery points are the most important 'intermediate customers', and they must receive the products they need. Their main concern is quality of care, and they depend on the logistics

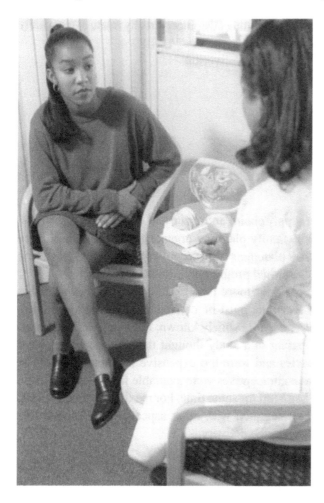

This young woman receiving family planning counselling expects her choice of contraceptives to be available when she needs it.

system to help meet their quality of care goals. Service providers expect the logistics system to deliver a dependable supply of quality contraceptives and other products for their clients with minimal extra work on the part of the providers.

Warehouses and stores in the distribution chain are also intermediate customers. Their expectations include logistics system resources (staff, storage space, and transport); regular, predictable resupply of all products from the next highest level; and technical support and problem-solving assistance, when needed.

Policy makers and senior programme managers need to be treated as customers by the next highest level in the system: donors, lenders, or other suppliers of products. Policy makers are important customers because they control the allocation of funds and other resources for the supply chain. As the first representatives of the country distribution system, their needs are the same as customers' along the supply chain: a reliable supply of the right products, at the right time. They also expect the logistics system to provide accurate data on stock levels, strict accountability for products, and cost-effective logistics operations.

International donors are the customers of their suppliers. Above all, donors want the logistics system to ensure the availability of contraceptives to all current and potential customers. They also expect the in-country logistics system to ensure accountability for donated products and to provide accurate, timely data on contraceptives consumed, quantities on hand, and quantities needed.

When a customer culture is developed within a contraceptive supply chain, all the system's customers and their respective needs and expectations must be identified. The primary customer, however, is always the family planning client. While a logistics system must satisfy a variety of internal or intermediate customers, the most successful supply chains unwaveringly focus on satisfying end users (see Figure 3.2).

Focusing on Customer Service in Commercial Logistics

> No customer should ever leave a clinic disappointed because the product he or she needs is out of stock.

A revolution took place in commercial logistics during the 1990s – logistics was seen as a direct link to the 'bottom line', a company's profitability or shareholder value. Superior logistics operations were seen as a way to gain competitive advantage and, consequently, to increase profits. The revolution centred on enhanced customer service. Intense focus on the customer became the hallmark of successful commercial logistics management. Now, logistics systems with strong customer cultures are common in the private sector. Supply chain management, once relegated to obscurity in most large businesses, but now a high-profile operation, receives close attention from senior management. Note how a recent major text describes these changes:

> Logistics is in the limelight. Once viewed by corporate executives, the business press, and Wall Street as a backroom function with about as much strategic

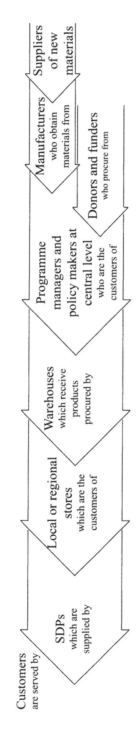

Figure 3.2   Supply chain diagram

impact as the mailroom, the delivery of raw materials and finished goods to their appointed destinations has gained new-found respect as a source of cost savings and competitive advantage. The topics of logistics and supply chain management are now centre stage in the executive suites of major corporations around the world. Logistics conferences today overflow with attendees once considered far removed from day-to-day logistics concerns in their companies – heads of marketing, customer service, finance, manufacturing, sales, research and development, and engineering (Keebler et al., 1999).

Focusing on Customer Service in Public Sector Logistics

Customer satisfaction has long been recognized as the key motivator in family planning programmes, but supply chain managers traditionally have

Whether conducting a mass vaccination day or launching a new contraceptive method, programme planners, promoters (in information, education, and communication [IEC]; media; and marketing units), and supply chain managers must work together from the outset to ensure adequate supplies for customers. Logistics has to be well integrated into the programme to ensure the best chance of success.

not focused on how their supply chains can satisfy customers. Even today, many family planning programme managers underestimate the links among a dependable contraceptive supply, satisfied clients, increased contraceptive prevalence and continuation rates, and improved programme efficiency.

Unlike the commercial sector's central focus on profit or, more accurately, shareholder value, a family planning organization or an MOH may undervalue logistics because it does not have a single, easily defined bottom line. Since the 1994 International Conference on Population and Development in Cairo, national family planning programmes have increasingly tried to identify clients as the bottom line, but public sector services will never depend on their customers in the same direct way businesses depend on their customers. Therefore, the important potential role of logistics may be hidden.

The role of logistics is also obscured because the logistics staff for family planning programmes are poorly integrated into the overall programme. They do not think of themselves as having customers or as serving the ultimate customer, the end user of contraceptives. They may not even think of themselves as part of a health service organization. Further contributing to poor job image, they usually do not receive formal training in modern, customer-focused logistics (LeMay and Carr et al., 1999).

Despite the challenges, to improve client satisfaction and programme performance in developing countries, a customer-oriented supply chain can and should be developed for family planning and health programmes.

Transferring Customer Orientation to Public Sector Logistics

Traditionally, health services have had a strong customer orientation – they exist to serve the patient or client. The philosophy of service is deeply ingrained in the health professions. While commercial enterprises depend on customers (sales) for survival in a way that an MOH does not, a family planning organization does depend on clients for its success, and the organization should strive for the highest level of client satisfaction, which can only be achieved one customer at a time. When policy makers recognize contraceptive availability as a key component of client satisfaction, they already have a customer orientation. But, they need to ensure that this orientation is practised throughout their organization – including in the supply chain.

Financial return in the commercial sector parallels programme results in the public sector: shareholder value motivates private business and programme results motivate family planning organizations. For example, a 10 per cent increase in the contraceptive prevalence rate potentially motivates a family planning programme the same as a 10 per cent increase in market share does for a private business. Likewise, a public health logistics system's cost-effectiveness and long-term sustainability parallel a private company's profitability and long-term survival.

Public sector logistics personnel, unlike their commercial sector counterparts, rarely receive salary increases or quick promotions as rewards for superior performance. However, public sector staff can be motivated to improve their performance and the performance of the system if they understand its real purpose and their link to positive social benefits. If staff believe in the organization and understand its mission, they are more likely to do a good job, meet and overcome challenges, and take pride in their work. The customer service philosophy can be applied to the public sector because many of the intangible, psychological rewards are common to all employees, whether in the private or public sector.

Parallels between the private and private sectors indicate that the customer service philosophy is transferable, with appropriate adaptations, to public sector and nongovernmental organizations' supply chain management. Client satisfaction as a value and goal is already well established in the health sector, suggesting that a customer culture can be established within contraceptive supply chains. The existing strong focus on client satisfaction in family planning programmes only needs to be broadened to include logistics operations.

As an example, in Burkina Faso, the central store had categorized two identical IUDs as different products; the only difference between the two was the manufacturer and packaging. In 1997, one of the IUD brands stocked out, and the central store placed an order for more supplies. Family planning customers were unhappy not to receive IUDs when they wanted them, and service providers were frustrated by the lack of supplies. Logistics workers, realizing the two products were the same, put both IUDs under the same code. Because of this intervention, back orders were quickly filled, customers found the supplies they wanted, and unnecessary emergency orders were cancelled.

Bringing it Together: Policy Makers' Perspective on Customer Service

Public health policy makers are committed to customer service. They may use a different term, such as quality of care, but they want to serve clients well. However, they may neither have an intuitive understanding of logistics'

In many countries, including Bangladesh, dedicated health workers often face flooded villages and other hazardous conditions when delivering contraceptive supplies to their customers.

Rehana, a family welfare assistant in Bangladesh, has family planning clients who depend on her for their contraceptive supplies. She takes her responsibilities very seriously. Rehana lives in a low-lying area that is usually covered with water during the rainy season. When she visits customers, she must carry contraceptives and record books wrapped in plastic to protect them from the water. She works long hours, travelling five days a week, often in a crowded boat, to give her customers oral contraceptives and condoms, and to escort them for IUDs and sterilization services. She talks to her clients and asks them about problems they may be having with their contraceptives. She records these problems and other pertinent issues in her book, and then discusses the issues with her supervisor. If necessary, she makes extra visits to her new IUD and sterilization clients.

role in customer service, nor understand that modern logistics management focuses wholly on the customer. Policy makers may need to combine these ideas for their programme staff and frame their expectations for the logistics system in customer service terms.

For example, to create a customer focus, policy makers should:

- decentralize decision-making authority so the logistics staff can solve a problem and take action quickly. For problems outside established procedures, allow staff to develop creative new schemes;
- ensure that managers set a good customer service example. Establishing a customer culture is a top-down process; senior managers must model good customer service behaviour.

Policy makers must understand that it takes a long time to instill a customer orientation within a public sector logistics system. Many contraceptive logistics systems have existed for decades as passive organizations, often with unmotivated staff. Typical MOH or NGO storekeepers, for example, understood their role to be to 'hold on to stock'. For them, the more stock they had on hand, the better they were performing. For storekeepers to accept that their real role is to move products to their ultimate customers – family planning clients – requires them to change how they view and perform their jobs. Instilling a customer orientation requires a thorough reorientation throughout the supply chain. It requires vision; careful planning; multiple interventions; patience; and, above all, persistence.

Practical Tips for Programme Managers: Instilling Customer Service within a Supply Chain

For programme managers who want to instill a customer focus in their supply chains, the following lessons, from field experiences in many countries, are essential.

Programme managers should:

- focus on contraceptive availability at all service delivery points, and at all times;
- understand the various types of customers in the family planning supply chain and identify their met and unmet needs. Develop strategies that meet intermediate and ultimate customers' needs;

- organize the supply chain to promote good customer service. For example, service organizations found that the more integrated the logistics system was with the programme planning, service delivery, and marketing and promotion aspects of the programme, the more responsive they were to customer requirements;
- create a logistics system with a customer culture where the logistics staff routinely ask customers what they want, listen to their customers, and communicate a genuine interest in the customers' concerns;
- train the logistics staff in technical and interpersonal skills to solve customers' problems and deal with the unexpected. Use training to reinforce the message that the logistics system works for customers. As skills in customer relations improve, staff's self-image gradually improves, performance improves, and the process reinforces itself;
- ask customers what they want – never assume – and don't ask just once. Customers change and their needs change, so they must be asked regularly, if only to confirm that the supply chain is dependably meeting their need for products;
- provide direct feedback from customers to supply chain staff and share the feedback up and down the supply chain to help staff see where progress has been made and where they need to improve. Without feedback, a customer culture cannot be established or maintained.

Chapter 4

People and Organizations: Improving Performance for a Stronger Supply Chain

In Brief

People make supply chains work effectively. When you improve staff performance, you improve organizational and logistics system performance and the availability of contraceptives. Managers of successful supply chains make a significant investment in staff, and they see the results in a high standard of customer service.

Everyone in a supply chain has a customer service role, and for the logistics system to function optimally, each person must be customer-oriented. Albrecht and Zemke (1990) explain: 'If you're not serving the customer, you had better be serving someone who is.'

In addition to building skills, programme managers should develop and maintain an environment that supports the work of the supply chain staff. When an organization promotes the growth of its staff and guarantees a supportive work environment, staff see their work as valuable; they are motivated and committed to the organization and its purpose – providing essential health products to the customer.

Effective organizations maintain the desired level of individual and organizational performance through training and other performance improvement interventions: supervision and monitoring systems, compensation plans, and technical support. Leaders guide the development and performance of their organization, making changes that enable the supply chain staff to excel in their work. This chapter focuses on how to keep the supply chain staff and organization working together to ensure customer satisfaction.

Who Are the Supply Chain Staff and Who Are Their Customers?

Recognizing that your customer is the next person in the supply chain differs from traditional bureaucracy.

Every employee – from dockworkers at the manufacturer to service providers at service delivery points – belongs to a long supply chain that ultimately provides a regular supply of essential health products to customers. For the supply chain to function effectively, everyone in this complex chain must perform specific logistics functions.

Because the organizing principle of contraceptive logistics is to serve the ultimate customer, supply chain staff must understand their particular roles. While service providers can easily understand how they are expected to serve the customer, storekeepers and other staff, with limited customer contact, may not understand their relationship and responsibility to the customer.

In fact, supply chain staff without direct client contact have different customers to consider. The district storekeeper's primary customer is the health centre provider who receives the products dispensed from the district store. Regional pharmacists' main customers are the district storekeepers who receive the supplies. While knowing that the mission of the logistics system is to serve

Countries can use large-scale training to make significant improvements. Storage guidelines can be taught and storage conditions improved at little or no cost – using first-to-expire, first-out and correctly stacking boxes.

the end user, all members of the supply chain staff must also define their customer service relationships and fulfil their responsibility to others in the chain.

Recognizing that your customer is the next person in the supply chain is a conceptual change from the bureaucratic viewpoint often found in public sector health service delivery organizations – challenging managers to create the customer service orientation within the supply chain. When a logistics system is first established, or improvements are made to the system, policy makers must communicate clearly the purpose of the supply chain to all members of the staff and inspire them to commit to the supply chain mission.

Providing What the Supply Chain Staff Need to Perform

Exceptional staff are the hallmark of superior supply chains worldwide. Improving staff performance inevitably improves logistics performance and, ultimately, improves the availability of essential products. Logistics system improvements often result from changes in organizational processes, which require supply chain staff to improve their skills and how they do their jobs. Logistics training can improve staff performance, but other factors besides training also influence performance, and they need to be considered.

> If staff are not trained to carry out logistics functions, it is unlikely that they will be able to perform those functions competently. In one African country undergoing health sector reform, the distribution system for contraceptives was combined with essential drugs. The task of managing contraceptive supplies was moved from the family health nurse at the district level to the district pharmacist or pharmacy technician, but they received no training in forecasting needs for family planning commodities and may not have considered such products as important as essential drugs. Thus, despite plentiful supplies of contraceptives at the central warehouse, the district-level stores have had stockouts of condoms. On the other hand, in Morocco, nearly all the supply chain staff are trained, despite personnel turnover of approximately 10 per cent per year. The Moroccan system is decentralized, and local-level staff control the stock levels. Successful, ongoing training eliminated the serious problems Morocco previously had with overstocks and expirations.

Thomas Gilbert, a leading expert in human performance, defined what a worker needs to do his job (Gilbert, 1978). To better serve customers, supply chain staff need job-related knowledge, skills, and tools; an appropriate environment; and motivation.

What components of human performance and the environment constrain the activities of a supply chain? Constraints could be related to both *the person* and *the environment*.

People working on the supply chain need:

- specific skills, knowledge, and attitudes that can be influenced or improved by training;
- capacity, including natural abilities, such as strength, and mental or emotional capacity;
- motivation, or the internal drive to succeed.

Environmental requirements include:

- Information, including data and instructions needed to perform a job;
- tools and settings, including equipment, physical space, and an appropriate social environment needed to do the job;
- incentives, including compensation, recognition, praise, and rewards.

To improve the performance of supply chain staff, effective programme managers consider all these performance factors.

It is important to remember that training is effective only when deficient skills and knowledge are the cause of the problem. Training alone cannot correct the structural and resource constraints that may undermine a supply chain; it can only ensure that staff possess the skills and knowledge to operate the system effectively. Effective performance is a product of both individual and organizational factors. The specific causes of inadequate performance must be identified, and specific solutions must be found.

Understanding the Performance Improvement Cycle

When the supply chain organization provides and supports an environment where staff have the tools, information, work settings, and incentives they need, staff can perform their jobs. But, when any components are deficient, it is difficult for them to carry out their primary job – serving the customer.

The performance improvement cycle offers a model for improving staff performance (see Figure 4.1). Policy makers probably will be involved in step 2, approving the interventions and strategy, and in step 4, evaluating the impact of the interventions.

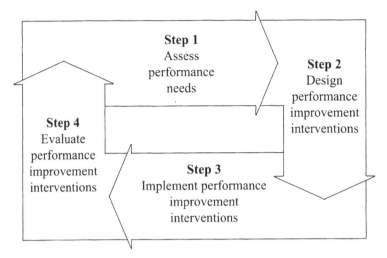

Figure 4.1   Performance improvement cycle

Step 1: Assess Performance Needs

The first step pinpoints skills, knowledge, environmental constraints or other weaknesses, and highlights anything that hinders the flow of products to customers.

Supply chain problems have many possible causes: obsolete vehicles and equipment, poor logistics management information system (LMIS) data, unrealistic delivery schedules, inadequate storage capacity, or incompetent logistics staff. Training is effective only when logistics problems are caused by the supply chain staff's lack of skills and knowledge.

Family planning organizations tend to regard logistics training as the solution to all supply chain problems, but training cannot correct problems related to insufficient infrastructure, misguided regulations or policies, or other aspects of the organizational environment. Unnecessary training can create cynicism. Staff may see training as unfairly assigning blame to them for organizational failures outside their control.

Before the performance needs of the individual can be determined, examine the organizational processes and identify the problems caused by the processes. If poor performance by the supply chain staff is the problem, the next step, a needs assessment, will determine if inadequate skills and knowledge are to blame. If poor staff performance is not the problem, training is not the solution.

Supply chain staff performance is evaluated against defined performance standards, ideally reflected in the worker's job description. In some cases, the standards are not clearly defined, and staff are unaware of management's expectations. People cannot perform a job they do not understand (WERC, 1997).

Interviews, observations, and surveys and questionnaires can be used to gather the information needed to assess organizational and individual performance.

Step 2: Design Performance Improvement Interventions

After the assessment is complete and the performance gaps are identified, organizational development or performance improvement specialists need to design appropriate performance improvement interventions, then develop a strategy to implement them.

The plan to overcome the deficiencies identified during the assessment (step 1) describes the proposed interventions – for example, classroom training, on-the-job training, improved supervision, job redesign, compensation, distance education, apprenticeships, and others. The performance improvement strategy usually includes a number of different interventions to be carried out during a specified period.

Step 2 also identifies the following:

- Who will implement the interventions?
- Who is the target of the interventions?
- What resources are required?
- Who will provide the resources?
- How will the interventions be monitored and evaluated?
- How will the changes in work processes and organizational structures be institutionalized and sustained?

If the performance improvement strategy includes training, the following questions are important:

- Who will be trained?
- Who will provide the training?
- What training interventions will be used?
- What resources are required?
- How long will the initial round of training last?
- How will the training be institutionalized?
- What continuing follow-up interventions will be required?
- How will the training strategy be evaluated?

Every organization must develop its own logistics training strategy appropriate to its needs, resources, timeframe, and objectives. At least five basic models have been successfully developed and implemented (see Figure 4.2) by different logistics systems around the world (Felling and Proper, 1993).

In Bolivia, the strategy to improve the logistics system included a variety of performance improvement interventions:

- Logistics workshops for health service staff: Ministry of Health, National Social Security Institute, and nongovernmental organizations.
- Trickle-down training strategy.
- Training of trainers workshops.
- Development and field application of the Logistics Supervision Tool.
- Development of job aids for logistics management tasks.
- Incorporation of logistics module and job aids for logistics management tasks in university nursing schools and technical auxiliary nursing school curricula.

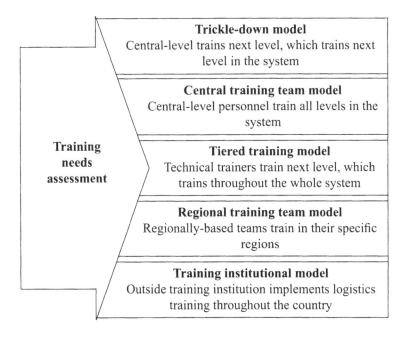

Figure 4.2   Training strategies

Step 3: Implement Performance Improvement Interventions

Appropriate staff, indicated by the strategy developed in step 2, undertake performance improvement interventions. When the intervention dictates a change in the work environment or incentive system, policy makers and programme managers are usually responsible. If the solution is training, local trainers usually conduct most of the logistics training after they complete a rigorous training of trainers course to ensure that they have:

- adequate technical knowledge of logistics;
- presentation skills and the ability to use participatory methodologies within competency-based training for adult learners;
- ability to use the logistics training curricula and support materials to present the content effectively to the trainees.

Experienced logistics trainers can also be borrowed from other countries or programmes. For example, two Moroccan master trainers helped training teams in Togo and Burkina Faso. They provided expertise and assistance and, in the process, learned new training techniques.

Step 4: Evaluate Performance Improvement Interventions

Evaluation is the fourth step in the cycle. At a minimum, it determines whether the intervention has improved the performance of the supply chain staff. The evaluation may be broadened to examine the impact of improved performance on moving supplies to customers – in this case, the evaluation expands to become a logistics system evaluation. This approach has the advantage of relating training and other performance interventions to the larger supply chain and its needs, some of which are unlikely to be connected to training.

The more in-depth the evaluation, the more likely you are to determine if the intervention had an effect on the performance of the individual and organization. One of the most widely used frameworks for classifying the effects of training defines four levels of evaluation (Kirkpatrick, 1996):

1 *reaction*: gauging what the participants think of the training programme – their level of satisfaction with the content of the training, materials used, trainers, physical facilities, food, and other aspects;

Trainers frequently participate in performance improvement interventions. Local trainers receive in-depth instruction in logistics training, including knowledge of subject matter, classroom skills aimed at adult learners, and effective use of materials.

2   *learning*: measuring how much of the training content (knowledge and abilities) the participants assimilated. This requires clear learning objectives for the training;
3   *behaviour*: determining how trainees' behaviour changes when they return to their jobs and how they put into practice what they have learned;
4   *results*: analysing the effects of the training on the organization or on the activities undertaken by the organization.

Obviously, if you are interested in improved organizational performance and customer service, levels 3 and 4 of this framework are the most relevant.

Evaluation is not the final step, but part of a continuing process. Evaluations provide information about changes in the content, process, and priority of the interventions tried, and they help to identify the need for reassessment and further refinement of the interventions.

In the Philippines, all rural health workers involved in family planning, including the village health station midwives, were trained to use a new LMIS. The new tool and training resulted in a marked improvement in the availability of supplies. An evaluation showed that there were no stockouts of oral contraceptives in the facilities visited in the provinces or cities (compared to 8 per cent that were stocked out two years earlier), and only 1 per cent were stocked out of condoms (compared to 52 per cent in the earlier study). The village health stations reported similar results.

Using Performance Improvement Interventions

Gone are the days when logistics training was seen as a separate activity with little direct connection to the overall performance of the organization. In recent years, training interventions have changed, shifting toward skills training and becoming more ambitious, aiming to impact measurably not only individual trainees' skills but overall supply chain operations, as well. This trend is most noticeable in the private sector where human resource issues are dominant in logistics. The commercial sector recognizes that training and encouraging its staff pays off in system performance, employee retention, motivation, and morale. The best logistics organizations invest heavily in staff development (LeMay and Carr, 1999).

Specific interventions can improve individual and overall supply chain performance by:

* *competency-based training*, a training methodology with an *expected level of competence* (ELOC) that all trainees are expected to achieve. ELOC, measurable and directly related to job requirements, is usually the minimum acceptable level of performance to ensure the smooth functioning of the contraceptive supply chain. Competency-based training formally tests all trainees and assumes that everyone eventually will achieve the expected level. Trainees not achieving the ELOC during the initial training receive follow-up support (on-the-job training or additional classroom training). Almost all logistics training uses some variation of the competency-based approach;
* *classroom training*, which includes formal training traditionally associated with lectures, but now employing a variety of training methodologies, including simulations and case studies. Simulations give learners an

In Morocco, 27 trainers participated in a logistics course and were subsequently certified. The new trainers trained and certified several dozen trainers, and those teams trained a total of 3,000 MOH staff in provinces and districts.

opportunity to *feel* what a particular situation is like; they are designed to be as close to real life as possible to enable trainees to relate the situation to their own work. Likewise, case studies attempt to create a life-like situation closely related to the trainee's own work situation. Cases, used extensively in clinical training, are effective for teaching contraceptive logistics to service providers, because health staff are usually familiar with this training approach. Classroom training works best when large numbers of staff are to be trained in a short period of time – for example, when a new logistics system is being implemented;

- *on-the-job training* (OJT), which is usually provided by a supervisor at the work site. OJT is most successful when the supervisor uses *job aids*, step-by-step instructions on how to perform a task. Job aids help the supervisor provide OJT and later serve as a reference guide for the worker. Classroom training is usually the most effective way to train large numbers of people; after basic training, OJT is the most appropriate performance improvement intervention to ensure that performance standards are maintained and continue to improve. Because supervisors often conduct the training, OJT strengthens logistics supervision.

Caution: An effective performance improvement strategy does not choose classroom training or OJT – both play an important role in performance improvement and both can be used simultaneously in most supply chains;

- *internships and apprenticeships*, or formal, sustained OJT, which pair a trainee with a more experienced logistics colleague to help the trainee acquire a set of skills through direct instruction, observation, and supervised practice. Internships and apprenticeships are appropriate performance improvement interventions for interrelated, relatively complex skills that cannot be taught easily in a classroom or to a group;
- *modelling*, which uses trainers or supervisors to demonstrate or model a desired logistics skill or behaviour, which learners later imitate. The

In Bangladesh, after classroom training in logistics, selected staff receive personalized on-the-job training (OJT). Using a checklist, field-based logistics support officers, trained in OJT, identify the performance requirements of the logistics staff during routine monitoring visits. Knowledge, skills, and job performance improve, and the logistics system performs better.

trainer acts out the desired behaviour in four to six easily observable steps; the steps are often filmed and shown so trainees can observe the same desired behaviour multiple times. Modelling has the disadvantage of requiring considerable time and effort to define the specific behaviours and create the training videos, but it is an especially appropriate performance improvement intervention for teaching 'soft' skills, such as interpersonal communications, styles of supervision, and customer relations;

- *study tours*, which are visits by policy makers and logistics operations staff to observe an unfamiliar supply chain and to learn lessons and practical approaches they can apply to their own logistics systems. Study tours are usually arranged to observe exemplary supply chains (those that manage to maintain a high level of product availability for customers). Follow-up is the key to successful study tours, first helping participants conceptualize and articulate what they observed, and then helping them apply it to their own supply chain operations. Study tours are an appropriate performance improvement intervention for policy makers and senior programme managers; they will benefit from the comprehensive overview of another logistics system and from discussions with colleagues who have successfully established an effective contraceptive supply chain. Even if the systems are not exactly alike, a study tour can enhance the visitors' thinking about the entire logistics process, the same way case studies are used in classroom training;

- *distance education*, which teaches skills and knowledge from a distance, using structured workbooks, with tutors providing regular feedback to trainees. The Internet has created opportunities for extensive use of distance education in logistics training. Distance education can improve the logistics knowledge of many staff from a wide geographical area, especially when it is difficult to bring the staff together for workshops or classroom training. Learners can stay at their duty stations; work at their own pace, at times convenient to them; and review materials as often as they like. However, distance education is resource-intensive (requiring, for example, computer equipment and Internet access for learners), and significant time, effort, and money are required to write and reproduce self-instructional texts, administer the programme, and provide timely feedback to trainees.

Caution: Distance education cannot stand alone, but must be combined with and supported by other performance improvement interventions.

Managers must find ways to compensate employees for outstanding performance. In the public sector, where financial bonuses and merit promotions are unusual, employees can be motivated by recognition from their organization and peers.

Sustaining Superior Performance

Training is only one of many interventions that can contribute to successful organizational and individual performance improvement efforts. Organizations often assign significant resources to the training component, but they do not always recognize the importance of other interventions. Without a variety of other interventions, training alone is unlikely to succeed.

Together with training events, individual performance is supported and sustained by:

• *compensation and reward system.* Effective organizations compensate their staff according to their organizational structure. For example, in organizations that use a teamwork model, it is common for part of the total compensation to be paid as salary and another part as incentive, depending on the teams' achievements. In the public sector, compensation usually includes salaries, housing, and other benefits, and is provided

Logistics training is most effective when it is based on a reference manual. In Jordan, 590 supply chain staff received a job procedures manual during training. One year after training, the staff said the manual was still a valuable on-the-job resource.

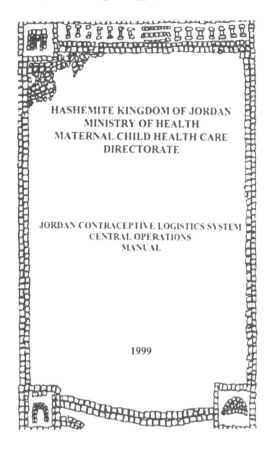

HASHEMITE KINGDOM OF JORDAN
MINISTRY OF HEALTH
MATERNAL CHILD HEALTH CARE
DIRECTORATE

JORDAN CONTRACEPTIVE LOGISTICS SYSTEM
CENTRAL OPERATIONS
MANUAL

1999

regardless of employee performance. A better system links pay raises or annual bonuses to individual performance, but this is not always possible in the public sector. In many cases, it is easier to reward outstanding performance outside the compensation system. Performance recognition can be as simple as an announcement of achievement at an annual or monthly employee meeting, or it can be more significant, such as additional paid vacation. One effective way to recognize superior performance is to give the high-achieving employee the opportunity to mentor others who may not be doing as well (WERC, 1999);

- *documentation of processes and procedures.* In thousands of cases, organizations invested considerable resources in training their staff in new processes and procedures, but they did not provide the corresponding documentation, and the desired results were not achieved. Job procedures manuals and other quick reference guides (job aids) effectively support

In Jordan, the senior logistics officer visits at least 25 per cent of the service delivery points in each directorate annually. Using information gathered during the visits and from the LMIS, she reports on how well each service delivery point is following the logistics system rules. The officer convenes a meeting of all midwives in the directorate and provides feedback, praising the staff service delivery points that have done good work and discussing areas that need improvement.

Staff appreciate being singled out for public praise; it provides positive motivation to those who receive it and to those who would like to receive it the next time!

formal training, ensure the consistency of the information provided, and contribute to the long-term institutionalization of new methods;
- *supervision and monitoring.* Performance improvement efforts do not end after a training course or other single intervention is completed. An effective supervisory system is one key to ensuring the desired impact and long-term results. For performance improvement to become part of the supervisory function, sufficient resources must be assigned for follow-up activities, and the staff in charge need to have the necessary knowledge and abilities. It is important for supervisory staff to receive training in supervisory techniques and methodology, in addition to training in technical aspects of the supply chain.

Supervisors are responsible for knowing not only their jobs, but also the jobs of the people they supervise. By observing staff in the workplace, supervisors can determine whether the employees have the knowledge, skills, tools, and environment to perform their jobs. A supervisory visit is most effective when the feedback is intended to improve performance, not to reprimand. Even employees who are performing well need supervision. In addition to giving supervisors the opportunity to observe staff practising their skills, supervisory visits provide a time for employees to talk about their work environment and renew their commitment to their jobs.

A well-designed information system can support face-to-face, on-the-job supervision. Using routine information system reports from lower levels, supervisors can monitor the performance of the supply chain and supply chain staff to determine where to focus their supervisory efforts. Supervisors can monitor routine reports for specific questions. Were the reports submitted on time? Were they accurate? Are there serious or consistent overstock or understock situations?

Bangladesh provided logistics management training to supervisory staff at all levels in the Directorate of Family Planning. When the supervisory staff make monitoring and supervisory visits, they apply their logistics knowledge and supervisory skills to check the stock levels and store records and to evaluate the storage conditions, using specially developed supervisory checklists and job aids. As a result, most of the sites practice good storage procedures, and stockouts of contraceptives in warehouses or at the local level are rare.

OJT is the main focus of the supervisory system. It is very cost-effective (compared to formal retraining) and responds to learning needs in an immediate, specific manner. Combined with job aids and other quick reference guides, whicvh the workers can use when they return to their jobs, OJT is an important performance improvement intervention;

- *institutionalization of performance improvement.* Any self-sustaining organizational improvement effort should focus on required abilities and technical knowledge, and the organization's capacity to design, implement,

In Jordan, the senior logistics officer frequently convenes meetings of all midwives in the directorate to provide feedback, discuss issues, and recognize well-performing staff and service delivery points.

> Practical training in logistics should be part of the professional education of service providers.

and follow-up performance improvement activities. To institutionalize this capability, it is crucial to include the training of trainers, recognizing the ongoing need for performance improvement specialists to conduct interventions. Creating local teams of logistics trainers can have a long-term impact on the process of organizational change. The trainers may be employed within the health or family planning organization, or specifically within the logistics system, or they may be part of a separate or auxiliary organization. Many models work well. The key is to ensure

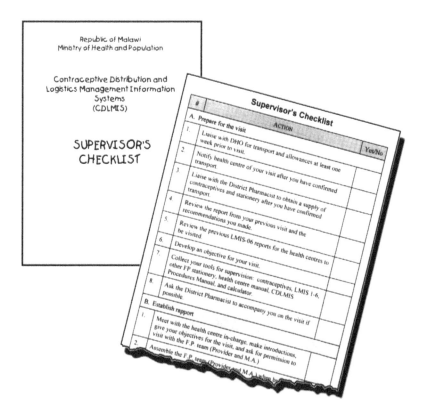

Checklists can ensure that essential details about logistics procedures are not forgotten during supervisory visits.

that the trainers can identify needs, formulate learning objectives, design activities to achieve these objectives, and conduct the activities.

In addition to institutionalizing the performance improvement capacity to support supply chain staff in the workplace, building logistics competence during pre-service education helps ensure the long-term sustainability of the supply chain. Beyond logistics theory, practical training in supply chain management for the family planning programme should be included in the curricula for the professional education of nurses, pharmacists, and administrators who will manage contraceptives as part of their jobs. For example, schools of nursing in Bolivia and Malawi are officially adding contraceptive distribution and the LMIS to the course curricula. Perhaps, in the future, professional associations of clinicians will recognize supply chain management as an integral part of health service providers' jobs, and require logistics competence for licensing, certification, or accreditation.

Changes in the health service environment – including health reform and decentralization – will demand that supply chain workers continually increase the level of their logistics skills. A prepared organization will be able to respond not only to today's reality, but also to the needs of an unknown future.

> Leaders in supply chain management create and communicate the mission and values of the organization.

Focusing on the Role of Leadership in the Supply Chain

Public health supply chains often focus on supervision and overlook the importance of leadership in creating an effective logistics system. Supply chain management requires visible, vocal leadership at all levels. Some logistics leaders occupy formal leadership positions (managers and supervisors); others are informal leaders whose job titles do not necessarily indicate their leadership role. In a long, complex supply chain, a series of strategically placed leaders, formal and informal, is required to keep contraceptives and other essential supplies moving through the system. Leaders set and communicate performance expectations and they model performance standards. They shape attitudes and behaviour within the supply chain. The key skill for every supply

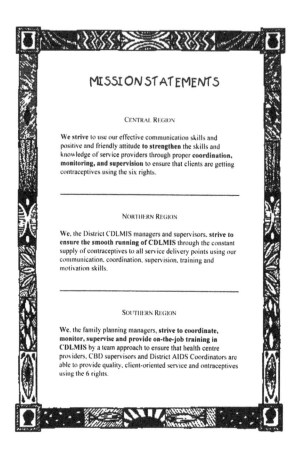

In a 1999 workshop in Malawi, regional- and district-level supervisors of the contraceptive supply system developed mission statements to inspire their work.

chain leader is knowing how to create and maintain a supportive, motivating environment that inspires staff to contribute their best energy and talents to serving customers up and down the supply chain.

Leaders in supply chain management, as in any business, are pivotal in creating and communicating the mission and values of the organization. Introducing and encouraging innovation is another important role of leaders. They have the power to either foster or squelch an environment that permits reasonable risk taking and innovation. Within a public sector bureaucracy, leadership is especially important when a supply chain switches from the traditional focus on goods to a focus on customers. Leaders strongly influence the way the supply chain functions; they need to be customer-oriented and able to relate day-to-day logistics operations to the ultimate customers. The role played by informal leaders is a vital part of this change process.

Because only limited real or sustained logistics improvement can be made without effective leadership, performance improvement programmes increasingly focus on the need to develop effective leaders in logistics.

Managers who want to become leaders should:

- improve their understanding of the supply chain as a mission-critical component of the larger organization;
- increase their ability to create and manage organizational change;
- expand their communication skills.

The most important decisions top logistics managers make relate to people – human resource decisions involving 'supervision, development, motivation, leadership, performance appraisal, staffing, organizational development, selection and recruiting' (LeMay and Carr, 1999). Every supply chain leader should know how to create and maintain a supportive, motivating environment that includes good quality of life and job satisfaction; and fosters high morale and commitment, high levels of energy and productivity, and a general sense of optimism and high expectations (Albrecht and Zemke 1990). The most senior leaders in the programme are expected to know whether these conditions exist in their organization:

- *quality of work life as reported by supply chain staff.* Job satisfaction, job security, salary and benefits, harmonious workplace, supportive supervision, opportunities for training and career development, and promotions;
- *morale of supply chain staff.* Commitment to their individual jobs and the overall logistics system and the customers it serves;
- *energy level of supply chain staff.* Active, industrious, and energetic performance of workers with enough reserve energy to take on new tasks or try new approaches;
- *optimism of supply chain staff.* A shared perception that the logistics system is getting better, a recognition of progress and improvements, and a constant striving for higher levels of achievement.

Leaders in a logistics organization must have the skills to analyse their work environment and then, if necessary, take action to improve it. If leaders believe that the supply chain staff want to do a good job and take pride in their work, leaders need to give them the opportunity to do so. In truth, the environment for public health supply chains is often weak. Leaders must have or develop the skills to repair the environment before lasting performance improvements in the supply chain can occur.

Bringing it Together: Policy Makers' Perspective on Performance Improvement

The policy makers' role in performance improvement is to:

- clearly state the strategy for providing a dependable supply of contraceptives and essential health products to customers and what each person is expected to contribute. Empower staff to act on this strategy at their workplace and to suggest improvements based on their experience;
- build a people-centred organization, visibly committed to the achievement of each person's best performance. Communicate clear overall performance expectations, consistent with the organization's vision;
- model and reward key behaviours. Maintain a standard of excellence in customer focus; treat colleagues, subordinates, and superiors fairly and professionally. Maintain an open, honest relationship with others in the organization; set a good example;
- develop leaders throughout the supply chain who know how to establish and maintain a supportive, motivating environment – an environment that inspires staff to contribute their best energy and talents to making the supply chain function effectively. Encourage these leaders to communicate to co-workers their enthusiasm for contraceptive and health logistics and their commitment to customers.

Practical Tips for Managers: How to Achieve Improved Performance

Programme managers can take key steps to improve performance and establish (or improve) a supportive environment within their supply chains, including the following:

- define the supply chain and the roles of the people who work in it. emphasize to staff that customers depend on their doing a good job;
- explicitly include supply management in the job descriptions of all personnel handling contraceptives and other essential health supplies;

- establish a mechanism for supervising supply chain staff and monitoring logistics operations. Provide feedback and on-the-job training. Recognize superior performance;
- identify and cultivate both formal and informal leaders at all levels of the supply chain, and encourage them to motivate their co-workers to develop a customer-focused supply chain.

Before implementing performance improvement interventions, do the following:

- clearly define the logistics system using officially approved policies, procedures, and forms. If the system is not yet defined, postpone interventions until it is;
- conduct a thorough assessment of performance requirements within the logistics system, including reviewing job descriptions and conducting task analyses. Identify required skills and knowledge, and the tools and environmental factors required for the system to function well;
- document supply chain processes and procedures. Ensure that the performance improvement staff develop a logistics procedures manual describing the logistics system, including job aids and samples of all logistics forms. Have staff use this manual as a text during training and as a reference after training;
- devise a strategy for institutionalizing the performance improvement capacity by training trainers in both logistics and training, and by including supply chain management in the curricula of health training schools or other pre-service training of supply chain staff.

Chapter 5

Logistics Management Information System: Tracking the Flow of Products to Customers

In Brief

Logistics data are collected, processed, and reported through a logistics management information system (LMIS), increasing the likelihood of an adequate supply of all products for all customers. An effective LMIS may be manual or computerized, collecting essential data about stock status and consumption. It ensures:

*   accountability for all products in the supply chain
*   a reduction in supply imbalances (stockouts and overstocks) at clinics and warehouses
*   efficient, cost-effective supply chain management.

To achieve these results, the LMIS provides decision-makers throughout the supply chain with accurate, timely, appropriate logistics data. Without these data, decision-makers do not know if products will be available when and where the customers need them.

LMIS data are used to control supply chain operations and regulate the flow of products from manufacturers to end users. In a family planning logistics system, contraceptives flow down the supply chain in response to LMIS information about consumption, stock levels, and customer preferences.

Why Logistics Data are Important

Because a contraceptive supply chain cannot function effectively without timely, accurate LMIS data, the LMIS is an essential tool for supply chain managers, customers, and policy makers. It provides managers with the information they need to react or, more important, the information they need to anticipate customers' requirements. In today's commercial world, logistics is more about the management of information than the management of goods (*The Washington Post*, 1999). Managers use information from the LMIS to ensure the continuous availability of products to satisfy their customers' demand.

Policy makers can and do use logistics data effectively. When one policy maker, Dr Sangala (Director of Preventive Medical Services, Ministry of Health, Malawi) redesigned his country's logistics system, he immediately realized how useful the information from the new system could be for communicating with donors. He noted: 'Without the new system, information about [contraceptive] consumption is not on my desk, and I doubt I have it. If donors should ask, I don't know the answers. It doesn't look right. It isn't right for donors to give without the satisfaction of knowing any more than vague ideas about how their commodities were used and without exact figures to back them up. If we had the information, it would be a simple matter of directing the information to those who need it.' As Dr Sangala discovered, donors may support programmes more willingly when the system ensures accountability.

In some former Soviet Union countries, contraceptives were traditionally scarce in the public sector system, and logistics data were not recorded or reported. When donors began providing contraceptives, no consumption data were available on which to base estimates of contraceptive need (except for the number of women with IUDs). Donations were determined by the estimated number of women of reproductive age. When contraceptive supplies arrived, they were divided and distributed solely by demographic data. Demand for oral contraceptives, for example, could have been higher in one region than another. Without better data, no one knew what the demand was or what the women's preferences were, so each region received proportionately the same quantity of each product, resulting in major supply imbalances – overstocks and understocks of different products.

An LMIS database can be used for more than managing day-to-day distribution of contraceptives; it can be manipulated for programmatic and managerial purposes that benefit the overall family planning programme. For example, Bangladesh has used its LMIS database to plan and monitor the introduction of a new low-dose pill, assess the impact of training activities, and plan storeroom construction. LMIS data can also be used to coordinate donor contributions, convince policy makers to allocate funds for contraceptive procurement, and monitor the impact of decentralization and other health reform initiatives on customers' behaviour. A fully automated LMIS database, a valuable asset for any MOH or family planning organization, provides policy makers and programme managers with hard data for making important policy and operations decisions.

For public health and family planning policy makers, an effective LMIS is especially important because it:

- *enhances customer service* by providing continuous feedback on the quantity of products being dispensed to users, tracking the number and location of customers being served, and directly linking the logistics system customers to supply chain decision-makers;
- *reduces commodity costs* by helping reduce loss, damage, and waste, and eliminating supply imbalances. An investment in an LMIS is recovered through improved cost-effectiveness for the overall supply system;
- *improves programme management* by allowing for continuous programme monitoring, optimal resource allocation, improved programme supervision and quality, and sound programmatic decision-making;
- *improves programme policy decisions* by providing data for decisions at any time, at any level, and in any amount of detail needed, unlike survey data. Moreover, logistics data can take the 'pulse' of programme performance: How many clients are being served? What are the trends in product preference?;
- *improves the accuracy of procurement decisions* by providing data about what products are actually in demand and used, helping managers avoid procuring unpopular or unnecessary products, or procuring inappropriate quantities;
- *provides better control and accountability* by enabling a programme to control the flow of contraceptives and other supplies, maintaining accountability for valuable supplies, and reporting the use of goods purchased with public funds and loans, or provided by donors.

Collecting Logistics Data

Because collecting data is time-consuming and costly, an LMIS should only collect the minimum amount of data needed to guarantee customers a reliable supply of contraceptives. Unfortunately, family planning programmes tend to collect far more data than they actually use to manage the programme effectively. Policy makers and programme managers must ensure that the LMIS collects data that will be used to make specific, identified decisions.

Contraceptive supply systems vary greatly in size and complexity, but the essential data captured and reported from each facility, at each level of the service system, are the same for all supply systems:

Staff in the Philippines enter only essential data in the contraceptive distribution logistics management system (CDLIMS), a management system that improves customer service and supply chain efficiency.

• stock on hand (quantity of usable contraceptives only);
• consumption (contraceptives dispensed to users);
• losses and adjustments (contraceptives removed due to expiry, theft, damage, etc., or transferred to another location);
• dates of orders/receipts;
• amounts on order.

The first three items are data recorded on stock records and aggregated or reported to higher levels. The last two items are data recorded for local use.

These simple data items comprise the core of every LMIS, providing the required information for all key logistics functions: forecasting, procurement, and distribution. The LMIS needs immediate improvement if it does not produce this minimal level of logistics information.

Stock on Hand Data

Stock on hand is the quantity of usable products of a specific brand available at a given place and time. To run an effective supply chain, managers must

Jordan Contraceptive Logistics System
MOH & HC Family Planning Program

Contraceptives

Stocked Out Facilities
Report Period: July, 1999
All Facility Types

Run Date: October 1,
Run Time: 2 43 PM

Jordan Contraceptive Logistics System
MOH & HC Family Planning Program

Run Date: October 12, 1999

Non Reporting Facilities
Program: Contraceptives
Report Date: January 1999

Type: MOH CPP
Phone:
Average Monthly Consumption: 41

QA-Ma'n Clinic

Code: W1Q01

Type: Health Center
Phone:
Average Monthly Consumption: 7

Type: Queen Alia Clinic
Contact: Jordan Hashemite Fund for Huma-
Phone:
FAX

Main
CEP

JOR

Type: Health Center
Phone:

Jordan Contraceptive Logistics System
MOH & HC Family Planning Program

Below Emergency Order Point
Report Period: August, 1999
All Facility Types

Run Date: October 1,
Run Time: 2 30 PM

Contraceptives

Supplier: Irbid Health Directorate

Condom

Type: Health Center
Phone:
Average Monthly Consumption: 187

Type: Health Center
Phone:
Average Monthly Consumption: 133

Jordan Contraceptive Logistics System
MOH & HC Family Planning Program

Over Stocked Facilities
Report Period: August, 1999
All Facility Types

Run Date: October 12, 1999
Run Time: 2 45 PM

Contraceptives

Supplier: Karak Health Directorate

Condom

Code: p1961
Name: Sarfa
Contact:

Type: Health Center
Phone:
Average Monthly Consumption: 31

Code: p1968
Name: Babr
Contact:

Type: Health Center
Phone:
Average Monthly Consumption: 7

Code: p1910
Name: Mohye
Contact:

Type: Health Center
Phone:
Average Monthly Consumption: 7

**HASHEMITE KINGDOM OF JORDAN
MINISTRY OF HEALTH
MATERNAL CHILD HEALTH CARE
DIRECTORATE**

**JORDAN CONTRACEPTIVE LOGISTICS SYSTEM
CENTRAL OPERATIONS
MANUAL**

Jordan Contraceptive Logistics System
MOH & HC Family Planning Program

Data Entry Error Report
Report Period: July, 1999

Run Date: October 13, 1999
Run Time: 1 52 PM   Page 1

Product	Opening	Receipts	Issues	Adjustments	Type	Closing	Avg Cons	Required	Received	New Users	Cont Users
Microgynon	0	0	0	0		0	0	0	0	0	0
Femplan	1462	330	130	12	I	1626	0	0	0	0	0
IUD	2231	0	111	261	I	2311	0	0	0	0	0
Condom	1899	13600	1775	5000	+	13964	0	0	0	0	0
Depoprovera	158	6	34	0		122	0	0	0	0	0
VFT	0	0	0	0		0	0	0	0	0	0
Norplant	0	0	0	0		0	0	0	0	0	0
LAM	0	0	0	0		0					

Jordan Contraceptive Logistics System
MOH & HC Family Planning Program

Supply Status Error Report
Report Period: May, 1999
All Facility Types

Run Date: October 13, 1999
Run Time: 12 41 PM

Stock Movement Report
Report Period: July, 1999

Run Date: October 13, 1999
Run Time: 12 37 PM   Page 1

Jordan's MOH recently introduced a new logistics system and LMIS for public sector and NGO providers of family planning services. The new LMIS collects and aggregates all the essential logistics data items: quantities dispensed to users; stock on hand at every level; and losses and adjustments. For central and district level managers, the LMIS also calculates the percentages of total programme quantities dispensed by each directorate.

know exactly what items are in stock, how much of each item is in stock, and where the stocks are located. Stock on hand data, aggregated for an entire programme, are used in forecasting and procurement planning. At lower levels, stock on hand data guide the innumerable distribution decisions needed to provide customers with a reliable contraceptive supply. Policy makers need to ensure that the LMIS collects accurate and timely stock on hand data and that supply chain managers use this information to make decisions.

Consumption Data

The consumption rate is the quantity of contraceptives actually given to users during a specified period of time. In LMIS terminology, these are 'dispensed to user' data, the foundation of an effective LMIS, and indeed of the entire supply system. Customers ultimately benefit from all logistics operations. Therefore, dispensed to user information is vital because it links customers directly to the supply chain. This strategy directly parallels state-of-the-art logistics in the commercial sector where accurate 'point of sale' data are collected, usually with barcode scanners at the time of purchase. Whether in the commercial or public health sector, *the top priority for every LMIS is to collect and report accurate consumption data.*

Issues Data

When dispensed to user data cannot be collected, stock issues data from the lowest possible level of the supply chain can be used (for example, the number of contraceptives issued from sub-regional stores to service delivery points or individual service providers). Using issues data as a substitute for dispensed to user data introduces additional uncertainty into supply chain operations because there is no direct information link to the real customers. Every effort should be made to modify the LMIS to collect dispensed to user data. Issues data, however, despite their shortcomings, are valuable for monitoring the supply chain, ensuring accountability, and, in some cases, verifying dispensed to user data.

Losses and Adjustments

In public health and family planning programmes, a stockout of an essential product may be a true life-or-death situation. A stockout could result in a maternal or child death, or a deadly illness. Because contraceptive stock should never be depleted, contraceptive logistics systems must maintain relatively large safety (or buffer) stocks. Contraceptive supply chains also maintain safety stocks because demand is often uncertain. The advantage of large safety stocks is that customers have an uninterrupted supply of contraceptives; the disadvantages are that money is tied up in inventory and storage, and stored products are susceptible to losses, such as expiry, damage, and theft. Although every system experiences some level of loss through expiry, excessive losses indicate poor supply chain management and should alert programme managers to investigate and take corrective action. The LMIS must collect and report losses so supply chain managers and policy makers will know if the system is functioning effectively.

A top priority for every LMIS is to collect and report accurate consumption data.

Even the best logistics systems may experience supply imbalances, for example, overstocks in some parts of the system and understocks in others. Logistics managers depend on LMIS data to help them correct supply imbalances by transferring commodities from overstocked to understocked locations; these appear as *adjustments* in the LMIS. Transferring commodities from a location that has too much stock to one that has too little stock indicates a well-functioning supply chain.

Dates of Orders/Receipts and Amounts on Order

Dated transaction records, usually called 'issue vouchers' or 'requisition and issue vouchers' govern the actual flow of product from one level to the next. To prevent shipments from being lost en route, both the facility sending a shipment and the facility receiving it should track the amount of product requested and whether or not the product was received. In addition, to calculate lead time, logistics managers should record the date each transaction was initiated and completed.

The following calculated data items are the basis for making other important decisions:

- *lead times* – the interval between the date a product is ordered and the date it is received and available for consumption is the lead time. To set maximum and minimum inventory levels and calculate when to reorder, a logistics manager must know lead times. If managers wait too long to reorder, a stockout is probable. If they order too soon, transportation resources may be wasted. LMIS data enable managers at all levels of the distribution network to calculate lead times;

- *months of supply on hand* – a well-designed LMIS converts the quantity of stock on hand for each product into months of stock on hand by comparing quantities to average consumption. This calculation simplifies decision-making: the fact that there are 1,254 condoms in stock does not suggest any obvious course of action. However, if 0.2 months of condoms are in stock, the logistics manager knows what action to take, particularly if the lead time is three months;
- *customer service levels* – LMIS stock balances provide an important measure of customer service. No stockouts at service delivery points means that clients have continuous access to the contraceptives they need.

In the Philippines, the CDLMIS quarterly Summary Delivery Report lists the facilities that were stocked out or understocked when they received their supplies, the percentage of facilities properly stocked, computational errors made by the delivery teams, and other situations that could be addressed and corrected at an early stage. The report is also a planning and monitoring tool, and is used to determine each location's supplies for the next delivery. The CDLMIS also calculates commodity usage at each site and level and for the entire country; evaluates the performance of both the delivery teams and the distribution system as a whole; and forecasts the country's contraceptive requirements for future procurement.

Recording and Reporting Logistics Data

LMIS data recording and reporting varies according to the design of the logistics system, number of reporting sites where data are aggregated, data processing capacity at each level, ease of communication among levels, and processes for inventory control decisions at each level. The goal of data recording and reporting, however, does not vary – to provide accurate, timely LMIS data from all the facilities in the supply chain.

LMIS data are recorded on:

- stock-keeping records (store ledgers, inventory control cards, bin cards);
- transaction records (requisition and issue vouchers, packing slips);
- consumption records (service records, daily activity registers).

Staff can be overwhelmed by excessive paperwork. The more burdensome the paperwork, the less likely that reports will be accurate or timely. Every information system should simplify its forms and streamline its reporting requirements to enable managers and service delivery staff to comply successfully.

All records should be easy to understand and use. To encourage 100 per cent recording and reporting, policy makers should ensure that no unnecessary data are recorded, recording forms are easy to fill out, and recording does not place undue burden on staff who maintain the records.

Sometimes forms can be combined to reduce paperwork for staff and still collect all the necessary data. In Paraguay, for example, the Contraceptive Movement and Consumption reporting form was revised to include data on new and continuing users, by brand. This change eliminated the need for two additional reporting forms.

Relieving busy staff of paperwork should always be a top priority; the heavier the paperwork burden (complicated forms, excessive data, many reports), the less likely it is that reports will be accurate or timely. When the Ministry of Health of Malawi and the National Family Planning Council conducted meetings to design a new logistics system, they wisely included staff from all levels of the system. On hearing some of the ambitious ideas for data collection and reporting in the new system, one clinic staff worker protested wearily, 'We are old bones'. Subsequently, they designed an efficient reporting system requiring minimal paperwork.

Most contraceptive LMISs rely on manual data recording, although some programmes are preparing to test automated approaches. Commercial logistics systems in developed countries make extensive use of hand-held computers for recording data, for example, stocktaking in warehouses or placing customer orders. These approaches may soon be adapted to large health and family planning supply chains.

Different LMISs use forms to report data at various times – daily, weekly, monthly, quarterly, and annually. Currently, almost all LMIS reporting is manual, although electronic reporting will increasingly become an option in countries with automated information systems.

Managers must provide incentives for staff who fill out and submit the LMIS reports. Linking reporting to resupply is the most effective incentive.

LMIS data reporting is a challenge, especially in developing countries with weak infrastructures. LMIS data usually move from lower to higher levels by reports submitted up the line on a fixed reporting timetable. Better results are obtained if reporting is linked to resupply, for example, when the quarterly report is also the request for new supplies. Another strategy is to gather LMIS data when supplies are delivered, reinforcing the link between reporting and resupply. In the Philippines, for example, permanent delivery teams simultaneously deliver supplies and collect LMIS data; the delivery team fills out the LMIS report for the receiving facility. This approach means that intermediate- and lower-level staff in the Philippines need less LMIS training and have more time available for service delivery.

Jamaica found that a 'topping up' delivery system was very effective for gathering logistics data and delivering the correct quantity of supplies. The delivery truck follows a regular schedule of visits every three months. The delivery technician: 1) does a physical count of supplies on hand; 2) calculates the average monthly consumption, based on the totals at the end of the last delivery visit; 3) calculates a new maximum stock level; and 4) 'tops up' the clinic stocks to that maximum level. This system depends on a regular schedule, carefully followed, and well-trained delivery technicians who know what to do in unusual situations that may change the consumption in the next interval (for example, seasonal variations in vacation areas).

To reach and maintain high LMIS reporting rates, managers must provide incentives for those filling out and submitting the LMIS reports. Linking resupply to LMIS reporting is the most obvious and effective incentive. Regular feedback reports also encourage lower levels to report regularly, and some programmes publicly recognize superior performance in LMIS reporting, rewarding conscientious staff with promotions, certificates of achievement, and opportunities for advanced logistics training.

Processing Logistics Data

LMIS data are processed, manually or by computer, to prepare logistics reports and orders. More sophisticated processing is required to calculate performance indicators, such as couple years of protection (CYP) and stockout rates.

At the intermediate and lower levels of a contraceptive supply chain, logistics data processing is almost always manual but, at the central level, computer processing is common. Manual processing works well with a small volume of data and simple reports. Computer processing is required as the data volume grows, or as reports become more complex and include

Hand-held computers can be used for stock taking in warehouses and for placing customers' orders.

performance indicators. Contraceptive logistics management has reached a level of sophistication where a computerized LMIS is almost essential for managing central supply functions – forecasting, procurement, and nationwide distribution. During the next decade, automation of LMIS data processing will probably be extended to regional and district levels.

Experiences from many countries show that LMIS software applications must be customized to the requirements for each programme, and that both hardware and software must be supported locally. Changing family planning priorities and method mixes, new organizational structures, and the evolving data needs of LMIS users require continual modifications in LMIS computer systems. Such modifications should be made locally.

In Colombia and Nicaragua, family planning organizations used local experts to develop software tailored to their specific needs and to provide them with ongoing support. A Bolivian company created the Contraceptive Monitoring Tool, which tracks commodities for all recipients of USAID contraceptive donations in Bolivia (more than 30 organizations); aggregates the data and produces quarterly reports on quantities dispensed to users, stock balances, and losses; and produces periodic reports. Programmes in Bangladesh, Ghana, Jordan, Kenya, Nepal, Peru, and Philippines have also used local experts to develop, customize, and support their LMIS software.

With appropriate automation, both the quantity and quality of logistics data improve dramatically. Automation of a manual LMIS adds value to supply chain operations by enabling more:

- products to be tracked;
- sites to be monitored regularly;
- data to be aggregated quickly, analysed, and made available to guide decision-making;
- feedback (timely and accurate) to be sent to lower levels and policy makers.

Before the new automated LMIS was introduced in Jordan, it took more than five months for annual data to be aggregated and presented to the Minister of Health. Today, within two weeks of receiving the last report, the new system can provide feedback reports about each directorate in the country and each service delivery site. Once a month, the senior logistics officer uses this information to communicate with the 21 directorates to identify stockouts, overstocking, and unusual losses and adjustments, resolving problems before they grow into crises.

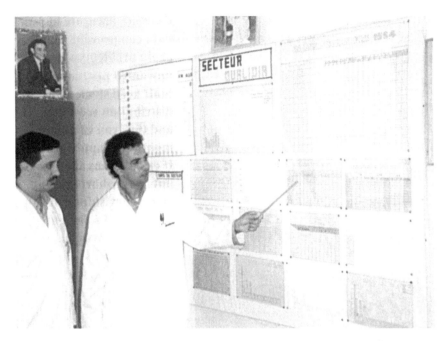

Manual processing of data works well with a small volume of data, but computer processing is needed when the volume of data increases.

After using a new manual LMIS for 18 months, the Social Security Institute of Mexico automated the system. The quality of the data has improved because dispensed to user data are required. If these consumption data are not collected and submitted on the reporting forms, the computer rejects the record. The form is sent back to the person who completed it, and he or she must enter the missing information.

Automation of LMISs is accelerating due to two common themes of health reform in many countries – decentralization and integration of contraceptive and pharmaceutical supply chains. Automation is the only way to manage the large number of products in an integrated supply chain. Decentralization will require computerized LMISs at provincial and district levels to provide the data needed for decision-making, on topics ranging from procurement to distribution.

Using Data to Drive Supply Chain Operations

The ultimate measure of an LMIS's success is how the data are used – by whom and for making what decisions. Recording and processing information

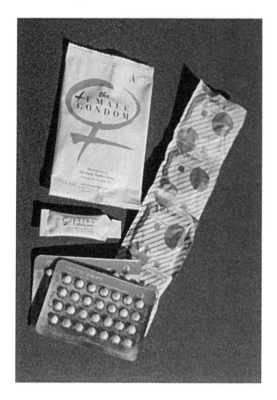

Current, accurate logistics data can prevent supply chain problems – and unwanted pregnancies. Staff keep stock and distribution records, and they can calculate months of supply on hand. If calculations show an imminent shortage, an emergency shipment can suffice until a regular delivery arrives.

is not a goal in itself, but a way to improve decision-making within a supply chain.

All effective supply chains have one thing in common – they are data-driven. Supply chain managers exercise good judgment, of course, but effective supply management is based on hard data. As family planning and health programmes expand and their supply chains grow more complex, customer service becomes more and more dependent on a logistics system guided by accurate LMIS data. Without these data, even the most experienced supply chain manager will be unable to guarantee customers a reliable supply of essential products.

Data for managing a supply chain are presented in LMIS reports tailored to the specific audiences that ultimately will use the information, for example, policy makers, programme managers, logistics officers, or storekeepers. Decision-makers will use accurate, timely logistics information only if it is presented appropriately.

The LMIS in Bangladesh produces a monthly logistics report for the warehouse managers' use when they make resupply decisions and plans. The system produces a monthly pipeline report showing the programme's stock status, shipments received and expected, and consumption. Central-level staff use this information to monitor supplies and shipments; plan procurement; and inform policy makers, who, in turn, use the information when they interact with donors. The LMIS also produces reports specifically tailored to the needs of programme managers (to monitor the stock situation in the stores they supervise) and supply officers (to determine what quantities to send to their stores).

LMIS data are used routinely within a supply chain to:

- identify stockouts that trigger immediate supervisory action and resupply;
- control distribution of products throughout the system;
- forecast and procure contraceptive requirements;
- track the movement of supplies;
- assess the adequacy of stock levels throughout the distribution network;
- monitor the percentage of facilities submitting LMIS reports;
- provide regular, action-oriented feedback to all reporting facilities;
- monitor trends in stock levels and quantities distributed;
- calculate CYP and other programme indicators.

As their systems improve, supply chain mangers will also be able to use LMIS data to:

- monitor customer satisfaction and customer service levels;
- measure and evaluate various aspects of supply chain performance;
- provide feedback for continuous supply chain improvement.

In the beginning, LMIS reports tend to be reactive; they are used to identify and respond to supply problems. As an LMIS matures, the reports enable managers to become more proactive, able to anticipate and prevent problems (see Table 5.1). Kenya's mature LMIS, for example, includes an automated Distribution resource planning (DRP) module that determines optimum delivery schedules and truck routings, based on projected stock levels at district warehouses. The Kenya LMIS helps supply chain managers anticipate and avoid problems rather than just respond to them. The goal of every LMIS is to use historical data to accurately anticipate current and future supply requirements and provide a reliable supply of contraceptives to customers.

Table 5.1   Information produced by a typical LMIS

Reports produced	Topics addressed	Target audience
Monthly highlights	Procurement, distribution	Top-level decision-makers of the MOH, NGOs, social marketing, and donors
Action list for the next month	Procurement, storage, distribution, transportation	Top-level decision-makers of the MOH, NGOs, social marketing, donors, and procuring agents
Preliminary findings of the current month	Procurement, storage, distribution, transportation	Top-level programme monitors of the MOH, NGOs, and donors; supply officers
Final findings of the previous month	Storage, distribution, transportation	Top-level programme monitors of the MOH, NGOs, and donors
Graphical presentation of contraceptive and selected MSR stock status	Distribution	Mid-level managers of the MOH and NGOs
Nationwide summary of contraceptive stock status	Distribution	Senior and mid-level managers of the MOH and NGOs
Storewise contraceptive stock status	Distribution	Monitors of the MOH, logistic personnel of warehouses and stores
Procurement and pipeline	Forecasting, procurement	Managers of procuring functions in the MOH, social marketing, donors, and procuring agents
Physical inventory findings	Storage, distribution	Monitors of the MOH, logistic personnel of warehouses and stores
Subdistrict stock status	Distribution	Subdistrict logistics personnel and supervisors

Note: MSR = medical surgical requisites.

Source: reprinted from Family Planning Logistics Management (1994), *Family Planning and MCH Logistics in Bangladesh: An Overview.*

Staff in Bangladesh use information from the LMIS reports to monitor stock in warehouses and stores.

Linking LMIS and the Health Information System

Health information systems (HIS) are essential to health service delivery organizations. Traditionally weak in developing countries, they are often targets for improvement. As they improve, the policy question inevitably arises: Why not merge the logistics MIS into an umbrella health information system? In other words, why not collect and process logistics data and health service data together?

Two technical issues – very different levels of detail and reporting frequency – make it difficult to combine an LMIS and HIS. Both issues result from the LMIS being an operational management system: it manages the flow of every product to every facility in the country. Therefore, the level of detail in the LMIS far exceeds what an HIS needs to or could collect. Moreover, logistics data are extremely time sensitive; they must be collected and reported within a short time (usually monthly) or the information is useless for the operational decisions that guarantee customers a reliable supply. In contrast, the HIS is a strategic, not operational, management system. Consequently, HIS data are

> The goal of every LMIS is to use historical data to accurately anticipate current and future supply requirements and to provide a reliable supply of contraceptives to customers.

far less time sensitive – data from the previous quarter or even the previous year may be sufficiently accurate and timely for the strategic decisions that policy makers face.

Thus, policy makers need to understand that these two information systems have different purposes, serve different users, and, therefore, have different operating requirements. Merging the two systems is rarely an appropriate strategy. However, linking the LMIS and the HIS is often a feasible alternative to a merger. For example, logistics indicators, such as a measure of total stockouts, are essential data items for the HIS, and an LMIS should be able to calculate and submit such indicators to the HIS on a regular schedule. However, the two systems must be linked carefully to preserve the integrity of the LMIS and the data it provides to supply chain managers.

Logistics staff are frequently authorized to 'over order' or 'under order', depending on the local season. During the rainy season, holidays and festivals, the school year, and other times, local staff must plan ahead to minimize stock imbalances and ensure a sufficient supply for their customers.

In many developing countries, LMISs are better developed and more sophisticated than HISs – often because the LMIS has benefited from donor support. In such countries, the LMIS may stand out as a model information system that naturally attracts the attention of policy makers who want to upgrade their HIS. It is tempting to assume that the procedures that work for the contraceptive LMIS will also work for HIS, and that by merging the two, the HIS will be pulled up to the higher LMIS standard of functionality. Some countries have tried to merge their LMIS and HIS functions, and while these efforts are still in progress, the experience to date has been that slower reporting and loss of vital logistics details compromise the LMIS. Instead of the more developed LMIS elevating the HIS to a higher standard of accuracy and timeliness, the LMIS is lowered to the HIS's standard, causing a decline in the availability of contraceptives.

Investment in the LMIS pays off in programmes' impact and efficiency.

Linking Contraceptive LMIS and Pharmaceutical LMIS

An increasing number of countries are integrating their contraceptive and pharmaceutical LMISs, two similar but traditionally separate information systems. The contraceptive LMIS is often better developed and more effective, but integrating two logistics information systems, no matter how unequal, is more likely to succeed than trying to merge an LMIS and HIS (see Table 5.2).

An LMIS that effectively tracks 5–10 items will not easily track 1,000 items. To do so, data processing capacity must be expanded greatly and data collection forms and procedures extensively modified. Maximum/minimum (max/min) inventory control, a standard component of most contraceptive logistics systems, can only operate effectively if products are normally in full supply. When products are not in full supply because of budgetary constraints – frequently the case with pharmaceuticals – max/min must be replaced by a rationing system. For this reason, the inventory control system for contraceptives is usually quite different from that used for pharmaceuticals. Another difference is that many pharmaceuticals are valuable and commercially desirable, which means the system handling them must help managers pay closer attention to accountability and security. Furthermore, some pharmaceuticals are legally controlled substances that may require special reporting and other special handling.

Table 5.2   Some differences between contraceptive and pharmaceutical systems

Contraceptives	Pharmaceuticals
LMIS tracks 5–10 products	LMIS tracks 300–2,000 products
Products are normally in full supply	Products frequently are not in full supply
Products are less commercially attractive	Products are commercially desirable
Products are politically sensitive	Products have greater political significance and support
Products are often donated or donor-funded	Products tend to be procured with local funds
Shelf life is usually five years	Shelf life of some products is significantly shorter
Storage requirements are similar for most contraceptives	Additional storage requirements include cool rooms, cold chain, and secure areas for valuable or controlled substances

One African country had a well-functioning LMIS that collected the dispensed to user data vital to successful family planning services. However, when the country underwent health sector reform and decentralized its services, the policy level decided to integrate contraceptive supplies into the essential drug supply system. This integration was announced suddenly and implemented quickly, without a pilot phase to identify possible problems. While the essential drug supply system may have been able to deliver contraceptive supplies to all the required locations, the information system did not collect dispensed to user data. The current data available are much less useful in calculating resupply quantities for each service delivery site and for forecasting the contraceptive needs for each location and the country as a whole. Now, resupply is based on issues data (quantities issued from warehouses to service delivery sites) instead of data on the actual quantities dispensed. With this new system, it is much more likely that the supply system will experience overstocks or stockouts of contraceptives.

Before integrating the contraceptive and pharmaceutical LMISs, policy makers should assess the purpose, users, and operating requirements of the two systems, and calculate the benefits in reduced costs and increased effectiveness in guaranteeing supplies for customers. One possible approach is gradual integration. Kenya's Ministry of Health developed a successful

> **Borrowing from the Private Sector:**
> **Distribution resource planning (DRP) in Kenya**
>
> Ten years ago, Kenya's family planning programme had no tracking system. Without accurate records, staff had to estimate the quantity of contraceptives to send to clinics. Some clinics suffered from contraceptive stockouts while others were overstocked to the point of expiry. In remote areas, stockouts could last for months.
>
> Kenya's MOH knew a lack of contraceptives could discourage customers from using clinics, leading to unwanted pregnancies, increased morbidity, and even mortality from unsafe abortions. The MOH needed a system to ensure that districts were adequently stocked at all times.
>
> The Kenya programme developed an innovative module for their computerized LMIS, called DRP, to streamline their resupply and transport planning efforts. When supplies are delivered to district stores, the MOH personnel collect information on stock levels and consumption. After recording the data on a simple, standardized form, they enter it into the DRP. The current estimated stocks at the districts are displayed and the DRP automatically updates the data. The programme also lists the quantities required by each district for a six-month maximum supply, and the final date the commodities can be delivered to prevent stocks from falling below a three-month minimum stock level. The DRP proposes the most efficient vehicle routing and produces a packing list.
>
> After software training, Kenya's MOH and health clinic staff used the DRP to reduce contraceptive stockouts and overstocking. The MOH did not limit the DRP's use to contraceptives, but converted the system to track some essential drugs and HIV/AIDS products as well.
>
> Using the DRP, Kenya has kept up with the burgeoning demand for family planning services. The modest investment in logistics resulted in substantial gains in family planning. Now, when customers in Kenya go to health clinics for contraceptives, they know the products they need will be available.

logistics system for its Division of Primary Health Care, including a well-functioning LMIS. Because it works so well, some members of the donor community requested that the Logistics Management Unit also distribute other items, such as drugs for treating sexually transmitted infections and HIV test kits. The logistics unit convenes regular logistics review meetings, attended by all donors, where progress on integration can be monitored and discussed. With careful planning, other health products can be integrated successfully into the contraceptive logistics system. Most countries, like Kenya, can link and eventually integrate their contraceptive and pharmaceutical LMISs.

Bringing it Together: Policy Makers' Perspective on LMIS

What does a policy maker need to know about logistics management information systems? Even the arcane details of data collection and management may be a policy concern. The policy level's important role is to ensure that:

- the programme collects all essential data, has simplified reporting procedures, and trains appropriate staff;
- programme managers use collected data for decision-making and reward data-based decision-making;
- policy makers use LMIS data when they make strategic decisions related to resource allocation, programme expansion, capital improvements, method mix, and donor coordination.

Practical Tips for Improving the LMIS

LMIS problems can be divided into three basic types: 1) design; 2) operation; and 3) use (Perry, 1994). For programme managers trying to improve their LMIS, the following guidelines, based on experience in more than 30 countries, may help.

Guidelines for LMIS Design

- Make the customer the focal point for the LMIS, giving the highest priority to collecting and reporting timely and accurate dispensed to user data, which will be used by logistics managers to operate the system effectively.
- Collect all essential data, and make the forms and reports easy to understand and use. Tailor data collection forms and schedules to the work flow of staff who will record and use the data; make reporting formats reflect the organization's management structure and the specific decisions the reports will support.
- Link LMIS reporting and resupply; consider collecting LMIS data when the supplies are delivered.
- Establish and document LMIS standards and reporting procedures; train to these standards and procedures, and supervise to ensure the standards are maintained.
- To minimize the risk of disruption in contraceptive availability, begin with a vertical contraceptive LMIS; later, expand incrementally to include

noncontraceptive items, maintaining the option of eventually merging with the pharmaceutical supply system.

- Customize a locally supported, programme-specific LMIS software application.
- Make LMIS improvement part of an overall supply chain improvement plan; avoid isolating the LMIS from the overall logistics system.
- Budget for the capital and recurring costs of LMIS design and implementation.

Guidelines for LMIS Operations

- Provide staff with the appropriate skills and knowledge to operate the LMIS; ensure competency through initial training, continuous retraining, supervision, and recognition of good work.
- Provide appropriate tools to operate the LMIS (computer hardware and software, forms, etc.).
- Establish a supervisory system to ensure completeness, accuracy, and timeliness of data recording and reporting.
- Monitor facilities for LMIS reporting, follow-up nonreporting, and consider giving recognition or incentives for regular reporting.

Guidelines for the Use of LMIS

- Use LMIS data to pinpoint stock problems (understocking, overstocking); develop a mechanism that triggers immediate action when a severe stock problem (stockout) is identified.
- Use stock status data to measure overall effectiveness of supply chain operations and identify location and duration of stockouts.
- Report LMIS data routinely back to each level in the system; assign central-level responsibility for encouraging and supporting the use of LMIS data at all levels.
- Report appropriate LMIS data regularly to the policy level; help policy makers use LMIS reports for their decision-making.
- Convert LMIS data into CYP and other measures of programme performance that are understandable and important to policy makers, programme managers, donors, and the public.
- Link LMIS and overall programme supervision to improve the logistics performance of staff throughout the supply chain.

Chapter 6

Forecasting and Procurement: Ensuring Timely Availability of Products

In Brief

Forecasting (estimating future consumption), procurement planning (estimating commodity requirements), and procurement (purchasing products) are significant, closely related supply chain functions.

- Accurate forecasting of future consumption is the first step in ensuring the timely availability of products.
- Procurement planning is the process of specifying the timing and quantities of products needed based on the forecast, desired stock levels, and amounts already in stock.
- Procurement or purchasing is the identification of suitable sources of supply and the acquisition of commodities according to a procurement plan, as economically as possible, within established quality standards.

After acceptable forecasts are made and a procurement plan is specified, the programme must obtain supplies from donors or purchase them from manufacturers. The procurement process is critical because contraceptives and other health commodities are expensive. Procurement managers must determine how scarce financial resources will be allocated, a process requiring transparent procedures and a trained staff.

What Are Forecasting and Procurement Planning?

Forecasting is estimating the quantity of each product that will be dispensed to customers (consumed) during a future period of time, usually two or more years; it is the starting point of a supply chain. To operate efficient supply chains that will guarantee their customers a dependable supply of quality contraceptives, drugs, and other essential products, health and family planning organizations need reasonably accurate forecasts of future consumption. Accurate forecasting of the contraceptives and other health supplies that customers are likely to consume is the only way to ensure that neither too many nor too few are ordered and moved through the supply chain. Too many products may overburden the distribution system; too few may create stockouts. Globally, the best logistics practitioners in the commercial, military, and public sectors know that accurate forecasting plays a critical role in creating an efficient supply chain, which ultimately provides customers with the products they need.

Procurement planning – specifying how much should be ordered and when products should be shipped during a defined future period of a year or more – ensures that the service delivery programme receives a continuous supply of contraceptives and other products.

Certain factors may cause procurement quantities to be too high or too low – budget constraints, product availability from manufacturers, introduction of new products, donor coordination, and natural disasters. However, by carefully managing forecasting and procurement planning, logistics managers can keep the pipeline properly filled.

A central warehouse in a West African country was overstocked with condoms, many stored in the yard because of limited warehouse space. When a large donated shipment of condoms arrived at customs, no one was anxious to get it cleared and delivered to the MOH. The entire shipment, put aside and forgotten, expired several years later and had to be destroyed.

Preparing a Commodity Forecast

At a minimum, forecasting for health and family planning commodities is an annual event, and ideally should cover a three-year period. Many country programmes review their forecasts every six months. More frequent forecasting may increase supply chain efficiency.

Policy makers, however, must weigh the advantages and disadvantages of more frequent forecasting. One advantage is that a year's forecast can be adjusted mid-year, based on actual – not projected – data. This increases the accuracy of the projections on which procurement and other supply chain decisions are based. Disadvantages are that more frequent forecasts require regular, accurate data analysis that may burden the logistics management team; and changes to the annual procurement plan may be costly and administratively difficult.

Three methods can be used for any type of forecast: setting a goal or target, exercising expert judgment, or using mathematical formulas (McKaskill 1999).

Mathematical forecasting is the most technically sound method of preparing an accurate basic forecast. The basic forecast is then evaluated and adjusted based on goals or judgments. Mathematical forecasting, a technically complex activity, often requires the assistance of experienced consultants. But rapidly improving computer software, data access, and local computer skills are quickly making mathematical forecasting methods user-friendly and locally sustainable.

> To operate efficient supply chains, health and family planning organizations must have reasonably accurate forecasts of future consumption.

To prepare a mathematical commodity forecast, you need information about your supply chain customers from one or more of the following sources:

1 *logistics data*: past quantities of each product dispensed to users over a specific period of time;
2 *service statistics data*: number of new clients and revisits, by product, over a specific period of time, multiplied by the dispensing protocol (the number of units supplied at a single visit);
3 *demographic data*: contraceptive prevalence or morbidity data and other population statistics.

In one Asian country, no one from the MOH was clearly designated to carry out contraceptive forecasting; therefore, sporadic forecasts were made by different agencies. Varied forecasts were produced, based on different sets of data, indicators, and programmatic input, making it difficult to develop a solid plan for the future. The MOH then developed a Forecasting Forum, headed by the Director General of the Division of Family Planning, which included professionals and representatives of the concerned units of the ministry, other government agencies (such as the census bureau), and donor agencies.

Today, the forum selects agencies or panels of experts to do the forecast, suggest method mix and future programmatic inputs and priorities, set the demographic parameters and indicators, review the short- and long-term forecasts, and recommend adjustments to the procurement plan. With these consensus data, the Division of Family Planning procurement and logistics managers work together to keep the pipeline full of essential products.

Family planning organizations are encouraged to prepare contraceptive forecasts based on all three types of data, followed by a reconciliation of the individual forecasts to produce a single forecast. This approach considers all relevant data and, therefore, increases the likelihood that the final consensus forecast will be accurate. If the quality of the different categories of data varies widely, the forecast that benefited from the most complete, accurate data is given the most weight in the reconciliation process.

Analysing trends in the historical data is the first step. The accuracy of mathematical forecasts is improved by factoring in: 1) observed trends and variations in consumption, for example, seasonal variations or a steady shift from one contraceptive method to another; and 2) future programme plans that might increase or decrease the demand for each item.

Given the importance of forecasting, family planning organizations are encouraged to:

- focus on collecting good data from reliable sources;
- assess the strengths and weaknesses of each type of data;
- adjust available data to compensate for missing reports and stockouts;
- factor in the effect of programme plans on consumption;
- reconcile the possible differences among forecasts derived from different types of data (John Snow Inc., 1995).

Every family planning or health service delivery programme needs to do forecasting for its essential commodities, no matter how small the programme or how few data are available. The forecasts will improve progressively from year to year as more data become available and staff gain confidence. The time and effort spent preparing reliable forecasts pays off in accurate procurement and, eventually, in timely availability of supplies for all customers.

Understanding Requirements Estimates and Procurement Planning

Forecasting predicts future consumption. However, the process does not stop there. A *requirements estimate* must be developed to determine how much to procure. The pipeline would be flooded if managers used only their forecasted consumption to procure and did not take into account what is already in the system and what may be on order.

Therefore, procurement plans are based on requirements estimates derived mathematically from the following data for each product:

- forecasts;
- stock on hand at all levels of the distribution system;
- previous procurement quantities ordered and dates expected;
- losses expected to occur due to damage or expiry;
- transfers to or from another logistics system;
- desired stock at the end of each planning period (including safety stocks and working stocks at all levels).

In a well-functioning supply chain, these data are routinely recorded and then reported by the LMIS. The estimated quantity of products required in a given planning period can be calculated using the formula in Table 6.1.

Table 6.1 Calculations for each planning period

Estimate of requirements	=	Stock on hand at all levels	+	Procurement quantities already ordered and expected	+	Transfers expected from outside sources
− Estimated consumption per forecast		− Losses and transfers to outside systems		− Desired stock at end of period		

What is Contraceptive Procurement?

Family planning organizations acquire contraceptives through purchase or donation. When contraceptives are donated, the donating agency does the procurement. However, the family planning organization will need to prepare a forecast and requirements estimate, and develop shipment schedules, discussed in earlier paragraphs. As countries become more self-reliant and procure their contraceptives using government funds instead of receiving donations, they must also develop and implement a procurement plan. This process may require competitive international tendering. Locally manufactured contraceptives are available in some countries (for example, in Indonesia, India, and Brazil). Whether the procurement process involves local or international bidding, policy makers, managers, and staff must understand how it works.

Procurement is the identification of suitable sources of supply and the acquisition of commodities according to a procurement plan, as economically as possible, within acceptable quality standards. Many public health organizations have experience procuring a broad array of products, but, as Table 6.2 illustrates, procuring contraceptives requires specialized knowledge and expertise.

Procuring Contraceptives Effectively and Efficiently

Effective procurement enables service providers to make contraceptives available based on the quality, timing, and quantity specifications in the procurement plan.

Efficient procurement means that contraceptives are available at the least possible cost to the programme and, ultimately, to the customer.

Centralized procurement is often recommended for contraceptives because:

- complex international tendering is best managed centrally;
- economies of scale and volume discounts reduce overall procurement costs;
- centralized payment often increases suppliers' confidence and encourages more bidders;
- centralized procurement facilitates quality control of goods entering the pipeline;

Table 6.2 Procuring contraceptives

Characteristics of contraceptives requiring specialized procurement skills	Skills required
Contraceptives (e.g., condoms) require special testing protocols and procedures	An understanding of testing protocols and knowledge of testing laboratories. Familiarity with national and international quality standards
Unlike other essential drugs, contraceptives (e.g., Norplant®) may not be available in generic form. Equivalent products may be available only under branded names	Knowledge of formulations and brands. Ability to draft specifications to maximize competition
Contraceptives are not manufactured in many developing countries. The scope for local purchasing at good prices may be limited	International purchasing skills, including international tendering, international contracts law, payment procedures, and others
There may be limited or even monopolistic or duopolistic suppliers of contraceptives	Advanced negotiating skills. Ability to access information on international market prices
The quantities purchased by the MOH may be small and unattractive to manufacturers	Negotiation skills. Knowledge of pooled procurement options Knowledge of bulk purchasing options
Brand preferences may be a major factor in clients' acceptance of methods	Knowledge of family planning programme considerations. Ability to collaborate with service delivery, and information education, and communication (IEC) components of the programme on issues related to branding

Many health bureaucracies are decentralizing their structures. Ultimately, the policy level decides if decentralized or centralized procurement is appropriate for a given programme. Even if countries decentralize most other areas, the overwhelming advantages in cost, quality, effectiveness, and efficiency may persuade policy makers to keep a centralized procurement process.

Managing Contraceptive Procurement

Contraceptives should be purchased from internationally or locally reputable suppliers. To do this, procurement managers obtain supplier references from agencies accustomed to procuring contraceptives (for example, UNFPA, International Planned Parenthood Federation [IPPF], and USAID). To ensure delivery of quality products with the maximum possible shelf life, they procure freshly manufactured products directly from the manufacturer, not from an intermediary. In the not-for-profit and government sectors, procurement professionals usually spend money from a sponsor's contributions, public fees, or taxes; therefore, the procurement activity must be transparent, including clear, regulated policies and procedures (Dobler and Burt, 1996).

Competitive procurement, as a purchasing method, can be easily translated into policies and procedures, and it is often used for the acquisition of contraceptives on international markets. Competitive procurement is defined as:

> Soliciting sealed bids from all or a selected group of suppliers based on clearly stated product specifications and quantities. The advantage of competitive procurement is lower unit costs due to competition. The disadvantages are that it requires a high level of procurement expertise and a long time (9–18 months) to complete the procurement cycle (United Nations Population Fund, 1993).

Some organizations may not have the experience to acquire contraceptives through Competitive procurement, and sometimes manufacturers may be unwilling to bid on the quantities required by a small programme. In these cases, the services of a reputable procurement agent (someone who conducts purchases on behalf of another organization) may be needed. UNFPA and Crown Agents, two well-known contraceptive procurement agents, offer volume discounts, arrange pre-shipment quality testing, and obtain preferential freight and insurance rates. Agents do charge handling fees.

> Whether local or international bidding is used, policy makers, managers, and staff must understand the procurement process.

Negotiating the Procurement Process

Typically, contraceptive procurement includes the following steps:

Step 1 Prepare procurement plan (develop product specifications, specify timing, and estimate quantities needed).
Step 2 Reconcile needs with funds.
Step 3 Select procurement method (for example, competitive international or local tender, or procurement agent).
Step 4 Select supplier(s).
Step 5 Specify terms and place order.
Step 6 Monitor order status.
Step 7 Receive and check goods.
Step 8 Make payment to supplier(s).

Completing all the steps in the procurement process can be time-consuming. It is important to know the total lead time required to procure contraceptives and to take steps early enough for the deliveries to follow the procurement plan. A 24-month procurement cycle is not unusual.

Many governments and donors have annual procurement cycles. They operate so that each of steps 1–8 occurs chronologically during the year, and the entire quantity arrives at the same time. This kind of cycle has the disadvantage of requiring the programme to hold large buffer stocks because deliveries are only made once a year. It is also difficult or impossible to adjust procurement quantities and delivery schedules with annual procurements only. Many programmes have found that a procurement cycle that is reviewed and adjusted quarterly or semi-annually works better.

Understanding Complicating Worldwide Trends

In recent years, contraceptive procurement has become more complex because of certain worldwide trends, which are expected to continue:

- total worldwide demand for contraceptives continues to rise each year; procurement systems are straining to keep pace with demand;
- the number of contraceptive donors has increased; procurement systems must work with multiple donors, each with separate requirements and procedures;
- the number of contraceptive manufacturers and suppliers has grown, especially those based in developing countries; procurement systems now have more choice but must pay closer attention to quality and reliability issues;
- manufacturing capacity and worldwide stocks of certain contraceptives (e.g., condoms) are low; procurement systems cannot necessarily depend on emergency procurements when unexpected shortages occur.

Bringing it Together: Policy Makers' Perspective on Forecasting, Procurement Planning, and Procurement

Forecasting and procurement are practical, hands-on activities, but the policy level contributes to the process in many ways. First and foremost, policy makers must understand the importance of forecasting and procurement planning. They must be aware of the long lead times in meeting supply needs; it may be two years or more between the time a supply need is identified and the time the product is actually delivered. Policy makers should take the following steps:

- integrate forecasting into the organization's routine management processes to ensure the long-term sustainability of forecasting for contraceptives and other essential supplies;
- build capacity in forecasting and procurement planning; designate and train staff responsible for these important functions;
- consider centralized purchasing to ensure quality and obtain the lowest unit costs, even if other logistics functions are decentralized to lower levels;
- ensure that reliable payment mechanisms and sound financial management are in place to support the procurement of contraceptive and health products;
- design transparent contraceptive procurement with documented processes and procedures and a published annual procurement report;
- establish a technical committee to oversee contraceptive and health product procurement. Coordinate donor contributions.

Practical Tips for Improving Forecasting and Procurement

For programme managers who want to improve contraceptive forecasting and procurement, the following guidelines, based on actual experiences in more than 30 countries, may be useful:

- strengthen the LMIS to capture the most accurate data possible on consumption, stock levels, transfers, and losses;
- involve family planning programme staff in forecasting and procurement planning; they are the best placed to analyse management information system data, and they know the impact of programme plans and how customers will react to various products;
- prepare forecasts using as many types of data as possible, followed by a reconciliation of the individual forecasts to produce a single, consensus forecast. Also, prepare high, medium, and low contraceptive forecasts. Obtain agreement from all key units within the family planning organization on a single forecast to guide all logistics activities;
- integrate forecasting into routine supply chain management. Forecasting is an ongoing process not a one-time activity;
- prepare a forecast for each product at least annually, but review semi-annually or quarterly after updating with the most recent LMIS data. At least once every six months, review your procurement plan against updated forecasts and current consumption data. Adjust quantities and shipment schedules, as appropriate;
- make product quality assurance an integral part of the procurement process;
- create one large procurement to be manufactured and delivered in scheduled partial shipments instead of smaller, more frequent procurements delivered in full or, least desirable of all, massive deliveries of quantities expected to last a year or more;
- procure competitively in bulk for the lowest prices; prequalify suppliers based on price and quality criteria before tendering;
- use a procurement agent if in-house capacity for international tendering is limited.

Chapter 7

Distribution: Delivering Products to Customers

In Brief

In a well-managed logistics system, warehouses, stores, and transportation form a seamless, integrated distribution network to deliver quality contraceptives and health products to customers at the lowest possible cost. Distribution systems operate best when they have the least levels necessary to effectively supply all service delivery points. The number of levels in an organization's distribution system does not need to parallel the administrative structure.

Policy makers must choose one of three approaches for contraceptive distribution: *push* (an allocation system), *pull* (a requisition system), or a combination of push and pull. All good health and family planning supply chains use the first-to-expire, first-out (FEFO) principle of inventory management. Most contraceptive distribution networks also use a maximum/minimum (max/min) inventory control system.

Good storekeeping practices and *dejunking* (eliminating accumulated clutter in stores), will increase usable space in a distribution network with little cost. Contracting distribution functions to private companies, especially transport, is a growing trend; it has the potential to reduce distribution costs, while simultaneously improving the availability of essential products.

Understanding the Contraceptive Distribution Network

Distribution traditionally refers to transporting products. In modern supply chain terminology, distribution includes both storage and transportation. Logistics managers now see facilities (warehouses and stores) and transportation as one integrated function in supply chain management. Integrated distribution focuses on *moving* supplies, not storing them.

A *distribution system* is the network of facilities where products are stored and distributed, coupled with transportation resources that move products through the network.

In Kenya's Ministry of Health, the Division of Family Health has a Logistics Management Unit (LMU) that distributes contraceptive commodities to all 60 district stores and 530 service delivery points. The carefully designed, well-maintained logistics management information system works in tandem with innovative computerized distribution resource planning software, developed locally by the LMU to plan the loading and routing of a five-truck fleet. Another important innovation of the distribution system is including drivers as an integral part of inventory management: they perform physical counts, check bin cards, and collect outstanding reports at the facilities on their routes. Distribution functions well, and logistics is recognized as a full partner in the health system, supported and trusted by the government of Kenya and all donors.

BIN CARD

No._____

Article _____

Date	RIV/IV-No.	Quantity			Signature
		Received	Issued	Balance	
(1)	(2)	(3)	(4)	(5)	(6)

Bin cards help warehouse workers keep track of products. Every logistics management information system (LMIS) incorporates bin cards and other stock-keeping records.

A major constraint for public sector contraceptive distribution is its reliance on government funding – government budgets are always uncertain and, in developing countries, are usually insufficient. Public sector supply chains unable to recover the full cost of their services are seen as a chronic drain on the health budget. The costs of logistics failure – unwanted births, sexually transmitted diseases, and abortions – are not as visible to policy makers as the recurrent costs of keeping the supply chain operating. Like the commercial sector, a public health distribution network needs to demonstrate its value to the overall programme to receive the support and resources it requires to perform optimally.

The goal of a family planning distribution system is to deliver quality contraceptives to customers at minimal cost. Distribution costs are sometimes estimated at 15 to 20 per cent of the value of the goods being handled (Marien, 1999). Note that such estimates can be misleading; depending on many variables, the actual percentage could be much higher or lower (Christopher, 1986). But, policy makers may use this 15 to 20 per cent rough estimate to check the cost-effectiveness of their current distribution systems.

Reducing Levels in the Distribution Network

In public sector supply chains, the contraceptive distribution system frequently is grafted onto the existing administrative structure. While this practice is often convenient administratively, there are more efficient ways to distribute contraceptives. In well-managed family planning organizations, policy makers ensure that distribution networks are based on functional, technical, and financial considerations, rather than political and administrative structures. Streamlining the supply chain can often yield substantial cost savings. With fewer levels, a full pipeline requires fewer products, and the stopping points for the supplies are reduced, so the products can reach the customer faster.

In 1989, the Ministry of Health and Family Welfare (MOHFW) in Bangladesh decided to streamline its family planning distribution system. Sixty-four district stores were abolished and replaced by 18 new warehouses, called district reserve stores. The central warehouse and three regional warehouses also began functioning as district reserve stores. Closing 64 district stores substantially reduced operating costs and increased efficiency. In 1997, the MOHFW commissioned an analysis of the distribution system, which found that a single national distribution facility could directly service all subdistricts with no intermediate tiers. The MOHFW is considering

> Seamless integrated distribution focuses on moving supplies, not storing them.

several recommendations that would radically reconfigure the distribution network while improving its cost-effectiveness (Family Planning Logistics Management 1997a).

To determine the minimum number of levels required, supply chain managers must consider the total pipeline length; desired frequency and speed of delivery; cost of transport, storage, handling, and inventory carrying; and operational constraints. These decisions always require compromises. The simplest, most cost-effective distribution network would have only two levels:

Central level   **Service delivery level**
A central warehouse for   ⇒ Service delivery points for receiving
storing, receiving and distributing   and dispensing to customers

In family planning distribution systems, managers must track costs carefully. Distribution costs alone are estimated to be 15 to 20 per cent of the value of the goods being handled.

In 1998, Burkina Faso's Department of Family Health eliminated one level in its distribution system, reducing the contraceptive pipeline from 21 to 19 months. This move streamlined procurement, reduced storage costs, and lowered the risk of expired stock.

In this distribution network, with no intermediate levels, the central warehouse delivers contraceptives directly to all service delivery points. However, even small family planning programmes may have hundreds of service delivery points, and large programmes may have thousands. Recognizing that a single, central-level warehouse cannot effectively supply thousands (or even hundreds) of service delivery points, most family planning organizations use a tiered distribution network with multiple levels. The typical contraceptive distribution network has three to five levels; for example, five levels might include central, regional, district, clinic, and community. Today, however, as transportation infrastructures improve and more attention is focused on cost-effectiveness, the trend is for contraceptive distribution networks to have fewer levels.

Many family planning policy makers face a common constraint – contraceptive distribution is frequently grafted onto existing administrative structures, resulting in too many levels in the distribution network. The more levels, the higher the distribution costs. If fewer levels can provide better service at less cost, the logic is clear. But institutionalizing that logic by redesigning the distribution system is a complicated, long-term process of organizational change.

Understanding Pull versus Push Distribution

Contraceptive supply chains use one of three distribution models:

- push or allocation;
- pull or requisition;
- combination of push and pull.

In a push system, the higher-level facility decides what contraceptives to push through the supply chain, how many to push, and when and where to push them. In a pull system, each lower-level facility pulls contraceptives through the supply chain by requisitioning (ordering) the required quantity at the time the contraceptives are needed. Both push and pull systems have advantages and disadvantages (see Table 7.1).

Both push and pull systems can work effectively. For example, Morocco's national logistics system is decentralized and the entire system is pull. The local level is responsible for avoiding stockouts and expiries. If local staff do not calculate order quantities correctly or order on time, they will stock out. In the Philippines, distribution is a push system; the central level makes allocations based on data received from the provinces and municipalities.

Neither push nor pull is inherently more effective or efficient for distributing contraceptives. For example, a programme with frequent staff turnover at lower levels is likely to push from higher levels to avoid constantly teaching new lower-level staff how to calculate order quantities. The heavy workloads of multipurpose community health workers may mean it is better to push contraceptives to them rather than expecting them to calculate their order quantities. In situations where demand chronically exceeds supply, a push system is required for rationing contraceptives among competing facilities and customers.

Conversely, a well-functioning pull system may have less waste, and it often fosters a greater sense of both responsibility and accountability among supply chain staff.

Policy makers sometimes favour pull systems because they seem democratic and encourage local decision-making. But, using pull or push

Table 7.1   Comparing push and pull systems

Type	Advantages	Disadvantages
Pull distribution	Fosters decentralized decision-making and local accountability Develops management skills at lower levels of the distribution network	Depends on good data and competent ordering decisions at lower levels Requires extensive training at lower levels to ensure competent ordering
Push distribution	Functions when rationing scarce supplies is necessary Functions even when lower-level management skills are weak, if data-processing capability at higher levels is strong	Reduces feelings of ownership and accountability at lower levels when decisions are centralized Depends on ability of higher-level facilities to respond quickly to unusual conditions at lower levels

should be a technical, not an ideological, decision, choosing the distribution system that will move contraceptives to customers in the most effective and efficient way, given local conditions, constraints, and requirements. In fact, many contraceptive distribution systems are a combination of pull and push. For example, regional warehouses may pull from the central store but push to health centres. In Nepal, essential items are pushed to facilities twice a year, but facilities can place supplementary orders to pull supplies if they run short. As policy makers decide whether to endorse push or pull, or a combination of the two, they need to ask the following questions:

- What logistics information is available at each level; what is the quality of this information?
- What are the logistics management skills at each level?
- How much time do staff at each level have for inventory management?

Generally, the best decisions on ordering contraceptives are made at the lowest level at which staff have the information, skills, and time to make accurate decisions. The guiding principle for policy makers is to select the system most likely to be effective and efficient in delivering contraceptives to customers.

Improving Storage Facilities

Storage facilities include central- and intermediate-level warehouses, storerooms, cabinets, desk drawers, and field workers' shoulder bags – wherever contraceptives and other health products are received, stored, handled, and issued. For policy makers, the important things to know about storage facilities are:

- Where are the facilities located?
- How are the facilities staffed?
- What items are routinely kept?
- What is the storage capacity?
- What are the storage conditions?
- How is the inventory controlled and kept safe?

A good storekeeping practice is to organize large warehouses by product velocity: products that move quickly are stored in the most accessible locations, while slower-moving items are stored at the back of the store or on the highest

Well-designed forms and procedures enable staff to follow whatever system is selected for distribution – push, pull, or a combination of the two.

GUIDELINES FOR PROPER STORAGE
OF HEALTH COMMODITIES

1. Clean and disinfect storeroom regularly.

2. Store health commodities in a dry, well-lit, and well-ventilated storeroom. Do not store in direct sunlight.

3. Secure storeroom from water penetration.

4. Make sure that fire safety equipment is available and accessible and that employees are trained to use it.

5. Store latex products away from electric motors and fluorescent lights.

6. Maintain cold storage, including a cold chain, for commodities that require it.

7. Keep narcotics and other controlled substances in a locked place.

8. Store flammable products separately with appropriate safety precautions.

9. Stack cartons at least 10 centimeters (4 inches) off the floor, 30 centimeters (1 foot) away from the walls and other stacks, and no more than 2.5 meters (8 feet) high.

10. Arrange cartons so that arrows point up (↑) and identification labels, expiry dates, and manufacturing dates are visible.

11. Store health commodities in a manner that facilitates "First Expiry, First Out" (FEFO) stock management.

12. Store health commodities away from insecticides, hazardous materials, old files, office supplies, and equipment.

13. Separate damaged or expired health commodities without delay and dispose of them in accordance with established procedures.

JSI·FPLM

The Family Planning Logistics Management project is a John Snow, Inc. project
funded by the United States Agency for International Development.
Contract number: CCP-C-00-95-00028-04

The key to effective stores management, illustrated on this poster, is to follow good storekeeping practices – maintain a clean, orderly store, adequate ventilation and light, segregation of caustic/flammable materials, and protection from water and pest damage.

shelves. Periodic, systematic dejunking – ridding stores of accumulated clutter – is a low-cost way to increase usable space and improve the overall functioning of the stores in a distribution network.

A prerequisite for effectively dejunking a storage facility is clear policies and regulations regarding the disposal of unnecessary, damaged, expired, or otherwise unusable products. Frequently, store managers fear they will suffer adverse consequences if they try to dispose of useless products.

Dejunking, discarding unusable products and items in stores, increases usable space and improves the stores' overall functioning, with minimal cost. After the dejunking is complete, standard procedures make it easier for staff to discontinue tracking and storing unusable products.

Procedures should be in place that encourage personnel to discontinue tracking and storing unusable products and that make it easy for staff to get official permission to dispose of the products. Unless staff are negligent, they should not be unfairly punished when they must remove or destroy unusable products.

Ensuring adequate storage facilities requires long-range planning, based on realistic forecasts of future consumption. Policy makers are finding that sometimes it is more cost-effective to lease storage facilities, especially warehouses, than to construct and maintain their own.

Overseeing Inventory Management

Inventory management comprises the procedures governing how supplies are received, stored, handled, and issued at the intermediate points in the supply chain.

Inventory management should ensure a continuous supply of needed products to customers while minimizing costs. Traditionally, the primary focus of contraceptive inventory management has been to provide continuous supply, not to reduce costs. For long-term sustainability, however, family planning and health organizations also need to focus on minimizing the costs of holding and handling inventory.

Contraceptives should be held as inventory for only four reasons. A supply chain that holds inventory for reasons other than the following can be streamlined:

- *transportation efficiency*: it would be unreasonable to ship a single packet of pills across the ocean or deliver Depo-Provera® to a clinic every day. For efficient delivery, contraceptives are held in inventory until they can be grouped into batches for shipment;
- *safety stocks*: supply chains are unpredictable – vehicles break down; consumption increases suddenly; and roads wash out, preventing resupply. Safety stocks are held as inventory so facilities do not run out of contraceptives when demand is unexpectedly high or deliveries are late;
- *limited storage capacity*: service delivery points closest to customers are often small facilities with limited storage space. In such situations, contraceptives are held as inventory at the next level up the supply chain, from which service delivery points can be replenished frequently;
- *anticipation of demand*: if, for any reason, the number of customers is expected to increase, contraceptives are stored as inventory in anticipation of the increased demand. Otherwise, the length of time between ordering supplies and receiving them may mean that stocks run out before the new supplies arrive.

Inventory records in a warehouse or storeroom, whether manual or automated, must include at least the following data:

- current stock level for each specific product;
- amount on order (pull systems only);
- historical data on all quantities received and issued, with dates;
- losses and adjustments.

Only with good justification should data beyond these basic items be included. Furthermore, routine reporting of inventory data to higher levels of the

In Niger, staff were confused about manufacture and expiry dates because products were not marked consistently. Written guidelines and training allowed staff to follow FEFO correctly.

supply chain should only occur if the data are necessary for procurement and distribution decisions. Inventory control systems frequently record unnecessary data and report excessive amounts of data upward.

Inventory control provides the necessary accountability as contraceptives flow down the supply chain, but staff time and paperwork may be costly. In some situations, it may be less expensive to accept a small amount of shrinkage (losses due to pilferage) rather than to maintain an elaborate inventory control system that attempts to eliminate all losses. In addition to being costly, complex systems often inhibit the flow of contraceptives to legitimate users. Zero shrinkage in a supply chain is an ideal that would be expensive, if not impossible, to achieve. Policy makers need to strike a balance among product availability, accountability, and cost.

FEFO inventory management ensures that products with the earliest expiry date are the first products to be issued. FEFO moves older stock first to prevent expiries in storage. The recommended inventory management method for contraceptives and other drugs at all levels of the distribution network, FEFO can be used from the central warehouse to individual service delivery points. The keys to a successful FEFO system are to:

- insist that manufacturers mark expiry dates prominently on all packaging;
- store products so expiry dates are clearly visible;
- train store personnel and their supervisors to use FEFO.

Max/min, an inventory management method, requires each facility to set maximum and minimum desired stock levels for each item. *Maximum stock levels* are set high enough to guarantee an adequate supply of a given product at all times during the ordering cycle, but low enough to prevent overstock and waste. *Minimum stock levels* are set as low as possible, but include a safety stock as a buffer against uncertainty, for example, if resupply is delayed or demand increases unexpectedly.

In most family planning programmes, max/min is the recommended inventory management method for providing a reliable, steady supply of contraceptives to customers. Max/min helps avoid shortages and overstocks at all facilities in a contraceptive supply chain.

Transportation links the facilities in the supply chain. Since most contraceptives move down through the supply chain, most transportation links are from higher to lower levels, culminating in distribution to service delivery points and then to customers. Some systems, however, operate on a come-and-get basis, where local transport is used to move up the system to obtain supplies. Transport links may also be supervisory links.

Because supplies move from higher to lower administrative levels, supervisory tasks can sometimes be combined with distribution tasks. Earlier, the family planning programme in one African country had the district mother and child health coordinators travel with the delivery trucks to make supervisory visits to the service delivery points and to ensure the delivery of adequate supplies. The system worked well, but it was changed during health sector reform, and the subsequent lack of consistent supervision had an adverse effect on the availability of contraceptives.

The more transport links into a facility, meaning the more sources of supply, the more complex the management of the facility and, therefore, the greater the likelihood of weaknesses or even breaks in the supply chain. Of course, the primary supply point – usually the central warehouse – necessarily receives contraceptives from multiple sources. At the lower levels of the distribution network, however, each facility usually is limited to receiving contraceptives through one link, possibly with a second link for emergency backup. Policy makers should be aware of the complexities posed by numerous transportation links, and logistics managers must have the following information to manage transport appropriately:

* How many transportation links does each facility have?
* What types of transport are used or available for use by each facility?
* What is the total carrying capacity of the transport?
* What is the travelling time between facilities?
* What size batch is cost-effective to transport?
* How often are shipments made?
* How do the seasons or weather affect answers to the previous questions?

Mr Ali Gabon, a nurse practitioner in Lamu District, Kenya, has really made a difference in the lives of people in his country. His one-man efforts in distribution have ensured an adequate supply of contraceptive products to even the most remote islands in the Lamu area. The Lamu District extends off the northeastern shores of Kenya, near the Somali border, and includes the main island of Lamu and a number of smaller isolated islands, accessible only by boat.

Bandits infest the roads leading to the Lamu area, so all trucks carrying supplies must have a security escort, which Ali arranges. During the monsoon season, trucks carrying family planning supplies wait four or more days until the rains end, until it is safe to load the boats. Occasionally, Ali, using his powers of persuasion, has been able to cadge transport on military, commercial, or missionary flights into Lamu's capital.

Once in Lamu, the supplies are transported by donkey or four-wheel cart to the local warehouse. Ali must then scour the docks to find boats returning to the remote outer islands and persuade the owners to carry needed supplies. Three to five months of supplies are sent on each trip.

The keys to effective transportation management are to:

* minimize the number of links in the distribution network;
* employ the appropriate type of transport;
* use optimum loading configurations to utilize each vehicle's capacity as fully as possible;
* plan delivery routes efficiently to maximize regular, complete coverage of all facilities;

- maintain vehicles through an effective preventive maintenance programme and proper supervision of drivers;
- minimize emergency orders by routinely delivering adequate quantities of contraceptives to all facilities in the network.

One potentially efficient transport strategy borrowed from the commercial sector is to avoid empty backhauls (having delivery vehicles make the return trip empty). If their transport planning capabilities are reliable, perhaps even MOH vehicles could be paid to haul cargo on their return trips from MOH sites. There are many obstacles to instituting such a concept, but it is something to think about!

In remote areas with poor transportation networks, supplies and products may be delivered by unusual means. In Lamu, off the shores of Kenya, donkeys and carts are vital transportation links.

The decentralized Moroccan system has creatively solved transportation problems by shipping boxes of contraceptives to service delivery points in local rural taxis instead of waiting for the MOH transport.

Contracting Distribution Functions to Private Companies

Transportation tends to be a bottleneck in public health supply chains. Vehicles are expensive to purchase and maintain, and shortages are common. Transport planning is often weak, and vehicle use is not easy to schedule, monitor, or control. Given these problems, policy makers may decide to use an alternative approach: contracting delivery to private carriers, or *outsourcing* transport. Done correctly, outsourcing reduces capital and recurrent expenditures while it improves availability of contraceptives. Done poorly, outsourcing can jeopardize the flow of essential health products and increase distribution costs. Contracting private carriers to deliver contraceptives is becoming more common.

Many distribution functions can be outsourced. For example, some public sector programmes use private clearing agents extensively for port clearance of contraceptives. The Government of Zambia recently contracted management of its central medical store to a private company.

Reducing costs is the main impetus for outsourcing. Another important factor is *core competency*. What is the core competency of a health or

A number of family planning programmes are successfully using private distribution companies for various programme functions. In Peru, the Ministry of Health contracted out transportation of contraceptives from the central level to the region, and despite the severe geographical obstacles, the system works well. In 1994, the Directorate of Family Planning (DFP) in Bangladesh experimented with using a private carrier to transport family planning and maternal and child health commodities. The DFP found it both cost-effective and cost-efficient, saving approximately 25 per cent in annual operating costs.

family planning service delivery organization? The answer should be service delivery. Transport should be the core competency for a transport company. By focusing on core competencies, each organization in the supply chain can serve customers better, if the different groups are well integrated.

Service departments, frustrated by chronically poor in-house distribution, tend to support outsourcing, as do contraceptive donors trying to improve contraceptive distribution. Resistance to contracting usually comes from entrenched civil servants who fear the loss of their power and jobs. However, few records indicate that public sector jobs were lost when distribution functions were outsourced to private companies. Usually, drivers and other personnel are absorbed into other government units, and administrative logistics personnel shift to monitoring the contractor.

To ensure smooth operations, a private contractor must be monitored constantly. The bidding and selection process for setting up a new contract can be lengthy and may lead to a lapse in coverage. Payments to the contractor must be made on time, or the commodities may not be delivered on schedule. Emergency deliveries can be costly.

Private carriers are more likely to be a viable option with a well-developed transportation infrastructure and enough well-managed private transport companies to ensure genuine competition for the contracts. Private carriers are usually the most competitive on high-traffic routes; therefore, policy makers may opt to contract for delivery from central to regional levels, but use programme vehicles to deliver to districts and below.

Cost determines when a distribution function should be contracted out, but the contractor's reputation and reliability, and security of contraceptives, are paramount considerations. The starting point for policy discussions, however, is an accurate cost comparison between the current in-house distribution system and the proposed contract.

Outsourcing is clearly a growing practice in health commodity distribution, and one that could reduce distribution costs while improving contraceptive availability.

Bringing it Together: Policy Makers' Perspective on Distribution

Distribution – including storage and transport – is the nuts-and-bolts component of logistics. Is there a role for policy makers in distribution? Yes! For a distribution system to effectively move needed contraceptives and health products through the supply chain to customers, many critical decisions must be made at the policy level.

Policy makers should consider the following:

* minimize the number of levels in the distribution network, while simultaneously increasing storage and management capacity at the remaining levels;
* separate contraceptive distribution from the administrative/political structure of the country if analyses indicate the potential for cost savings and increased effectiveness;
* determine the cost-effectiveness of the current distribution system. When limited resources must cover the commodities and services themselves, policy makers must know if the distribution system costs too much and, if so, take steps to streamline it;
* investigate the potential cost savings of outsourcing some distribution functions, such as transport or storage.

Realistically, public sector policy makers may not have the freedom to make such changes without a political struggle. If a customer-oriented and cost-effective supply chain is the objective, distribution system decisions will be clearer.

Practical Tips for Improving Distribution

Frontline programme and logistics managers trying to improve distribution should find the following tips helpful:

- treat storage and transportation as one integrated distribution function, with the emphasis not on storing contraceptives, but on moving them to customers as quickly and efficiently as possible;
- hang durable, plastic wall charts outlining good storage practices in all warehouses and storerooms throughout the distribution network; translate the charts into local languages;
- use dejunking – eliminating clutter – as a low cost way to increase usable space and the stores' efficiency. Have clear policies regarding disposal of unnecessary and unusable materials;
- determine whether pull, push, or a combination of the two, is the most appropriate for contraceptive distribution. Use push when demand chronically exceeds supply;
- conduct spot checks to ensure that facilities are keeping accurate, up-to-date inventory records and are using FEFO for distribution;
- use max/min procedures to manage inventory;
- determine whether the distribution network is holding stock in excess of maximum levels, unnecessarily raising handling costs and clogging the network;
- ensure that delivery vehicles are adequately monitored and controlled. Minimize the number of transport links within the distribution network.

Chapter 8

Transforming Your Supply Chain: From As-is to Could-be

In Brief

Is it time for your logistics operation to become a supply chain based on the ideals described in the preceding chapters? How can you design a more customer-focused, agile, and responsive system? What improvements will bring about more efficient delivery of products, enabling programmes to deliver cost-effective results? Can you create a more satisfying place for staff to work?

The transformation process begins with the correct diagnosis of your existing system, the as-is state. You determine what processes to preserve, modify, eliminate, or add to attain the could-be state that exemplifies the vision of moving goods through the supply chain to customers at the lowest cost, fastest speed, and highest quality possible (Kuglin, 1998).

Managing the change process requires the identification and use of a few appropriate metrics to measure your system's performance. Business scholars say: 'You cannot control what you don't measure.' You must measure certain key things, not everything. You need to know if your system is meeting its objectives, serving its customers, and showing improvement.

How to Diagnose a Logistics System

Improving your logistics system begins with correctly diagnosing the current or as-is state. You need to look at existing processes, technologies, policies, and linkages. Once identified, they can be compared with the desired future or could-be state. Policy makers and managers can address the gaps with specific action plans aimed at improving operations, infrastructure, and management (Kuglin, 1998).

However, public health policy makers do not need to become supply chain management experts to judge the overall effectiveness of their logistics operations. The essential measure of a family planning supply chain's

Assessing how well a logistics system operates involves data collection and analysis, as well as informed judgments by knowledgeable staff and consultants.

success is the availability of contraceptives. Therefore, the first question for a policy maker to ask is: 'Do *all* customers enjoy a *dependable supply* of the contraceptives of *their choice* at a place *convenient* to them?'

Regardless of the supply chain's current problems or state of development, contraceptive availability can always be improved, and the customer can always be given better service. To get a complete picture of the design and function of a logistics system, you will need to use an assessment instrument – a set of written guidelines to help you remember the many aspects and dimensions of your system. While the assessment process may be formal or informal, it must be comprehensive; it must look at all elements of a system and all levels of operations. The assessment's accuracy will depend on whether you incorporate the judgment of knowledgeable individuals – and customers!

By answering the questions in the following sections and gathering relevant information, you as policy makers will be able to describe the as-is state of your logistics system (Family Planning Logistics Management, 1995a). For many of these questions, answering 'I don't know' may reveal that the policy level is not sufficiently aware of logistics' mission-critical importance to their programmes, and is not sufficiently engaged in supporting, leading, and setting high expectations for the supply chain.

Customer Service

- Do you have a customer-focused vision statement for your organization and a mission statement for your logistics system? Does it specifically state that essential health and family planning supplies must be reliably available for customers?
- Have you identified any products that your programmes are committed to keeping available at all times, to all customers (for example, contraceptives, vaccines, and a short list of essential pharmaceuticals)?
- Does the programme track how well customers are being supplied with the contraceptives they want? Are customer satisfaction and customer service standards measured regularly?
- How often do customers leave service delivery points without the product they came in for?
- How often are facilities stocked out at any level?

LMIS

- Does the logistics management information system (LMIS) contain the beginning inventory balance, supplies received, supplies issued, ending inventory balance, and system losses?
- Do workers keep appropriate records throughout the system, for all contraceptives (by brand) and other essential health products?
- Does the LMIS gather, aggregate, and report consumption data?
- Is the LMIS documented in writing?
- What percentage of all facilities report LMIS data regularly and accurately?
- Is LMIS information used for continuous monitoring of supplies, orders, and forecasts? Is an action-oriented LMIS feedback report provided to all reporting facilities? Do reported stockouts in these feedback reports trigger immediate supervisory action?

Do all customers enjoy a dependable supply of the contraceptives of their choice at a place convenient to them?

- Is logistics information reported to and used by policy makers and senior managers? Is an LMIS report that shows trends in contraceptive consumption and stock levels produced annually? Is the report user-friendly with clear graphics? Is it circulated to all stakeholders?
- Are commodity data periodically crosschecked against service statistics, survey data, and physical audits?

Forecasting and Procurement

- Are periodic short- and medium-term consumption forecasts prepared, updated, and validated for every programme, commodity, and brand?
- Are projections of the cost of goods, warehousing, and transport included in programme cost analyses and budgetary planning?
- Do procurement plans take into account inventory levels, shipment and handling schedules, and anticipated changes in programme activity?
- Do programme managers know and comply with procedures and timeframes for ordering commodities from suppliers and donors, including trade, regulatory, and currency restrictions?
- Does the programme actively monitor and manage coordination of donors and suppliers to ensure continuous supply?

Getting into the field to check on logistics operations at every level is an important part of diagnosing the system's as-is state.

Warehousing and Storage

- Is storage capacity large enough to meet current needs, and does the programme have plans to meet foreseeable future needs?
- Do storage conditions meet acceptable standards, including guidelines for cleanliness; orderliness; arrangement and labelling of supplies to facilitate first-to-expire, first-out (FEFO); security; ventilation; light; fire safety; and pest and water precautions?
- Are physical inventories conducted at least annually at all storage sites?
- Does the programme have and comply with procedures for assuring product quality, including verifying that received products meet procurement specifications; visually inspecting goods; sampling and testing, when required; destroying unusable products; and capturing customer complaints about product quality?
- Are all stocks issued according to FEFO stock management procedures?

People make the logistics system function. They need the appropriate skills, genuine motivation, up-to-date tools, and suitable work settings to perform their jobs correctly.

Distribution and Transport

- Can you accurately describe the *push* and *pull* links between levels in your distribution system? Are they working effectively?
- Does the distribution system have and comply with regular procedures to restock each level, such as maximum/minimum or topping up? Does every level maintain inventories according to those procedures?
- What is the severity and duration of overstock and understock situations?
- Does each warehouse and store dejunk at least once each year (clear out all obsolete, expired, unusable items that clutter the store and reduce the amount of usable storage space)?
- Have stockouts occurred during the previous year? What products and brands were stocked out? How often did the stockouts occur? At what levels or locations did the stockouts occur? How long did the stockouts last?
- Does the system track and document losses and investigate nonroutine or large quantities of unaccounted for supplies?
- Do adequate transportation resources exist? Are they used effectively and maintained adequately? Has distribution suffered serious transport-related disruptions?

Organization and Staffing

- Does the organization have a logistics unit? Does it have adequate human and financial resources? Are personnel performing appropriate logistics activities?
- Does a dedicated, senior logistics manager have overall responsibility for managing supplies to meet programme objectives? Does the manager in charge have sufficient authority?
- What is the quality of supervision at all levels? Are job expectations, performance, and supervision based on written procedures and policies (for example, a system manual)?
- Do staff in the supply chain (including service providers) have adequate logistics management skills to perform their various jobs in forecasting, requisitioning, storekeeping, inventory control, distribution, supervision, and LMIS reporting?
- Is there a permanent, ongoing, sustainable performance improvement programme for supply chain staff at all levels of the distribution system? Have active personnel been trained in logistics?

- How severe is staff turnover, and how is it handled?
- Is logistics included in all pre-service and in-service curricula used for the various health cadres?

Policy and Adaptability

- Is logistics information provided to appropriate policy-level decision-makers both inside and outside the organization (for example, the MOH, Ministry of Finance, and donors)?
- What factors in the local, national, and international environment affect the logistics system and the availability of essential supplies? Can the logistics organization adapt to changing situations?
- Are donors relied on for contraceptives or other products, or logistics technical assistance? Is there a long-term financial sustainability plan for locally funding all contraceptive purchases and related logistics services?
- Can the system obtain resources, either internally or externally, to supply growing demand?

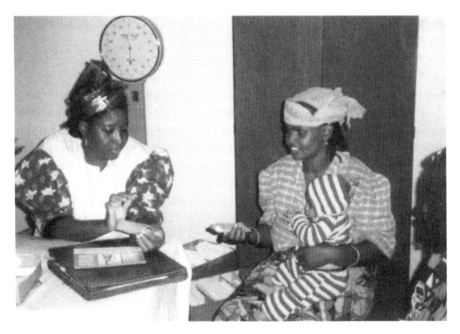

Ultimately, making products reliably available to customers is what logistics is all about.

What to Measure in the Supply Chain

While much has been written in the past decade about measuring supply chain performance in developed countries, no performance indicators apply to every organization (Keebler et al., 1999). The actual metrics adopted by a supply chain depend upon its unique strategy. Measures include, for example, return on investment and other cost-based metrics, inventory levels, timely response, perfect orders, stockout rates, forecast accuracy, and customer satisfaction (Brewer and Speh, 2000).

Limited literature exists on supply chain management in developing countries, and even less information about public health supply chains is available (McGregor and Chandani, 2000). For such systems, with their mandate to support programmes that deliver quality services efficiently to everyone, the key or first indicator is the continuous availability of supplies, as measured by the *duration and frequency of stockouts at the level of the service delivery point, by brand.*

The advantage of this indicator on stockouts is that a good LMIS routinely gathers the data necessary to measure it. This indicator can also be assessed by periodic stock-level surveys and client exit interviews at service delivery points. It is a particularly valuable measure because it is directly tied to the customer service purpose of any logistics system.

At the same time, measurements that indicate greater cost awareness need to be identified and used more frequently by public sector logistics practitioners in developing countries. To improve cost-effectiveness, the total costs of obtaining supplies and delivering them to the ultimate customers must be known and monitored. Retail supply chains understand that their bottom line is directly affected by how efficient their logistics operations are; public health service organizations do not necessarily share this understanding, particularly where products are donated (McGregor and Chandani, 2000). It would be wise for a programme to identify and monitor at least one cost-related indicator, such as:

- logistics costs as a percentage of the value of commodities in the system; or
- logistics costs as a percentage of total programme costs.

The cost-related indicators are far more difficult to assess routinely, but it is important to know and monitor them (using periodic special analyses, if necessary). Special cost-study methodologies have been used in different

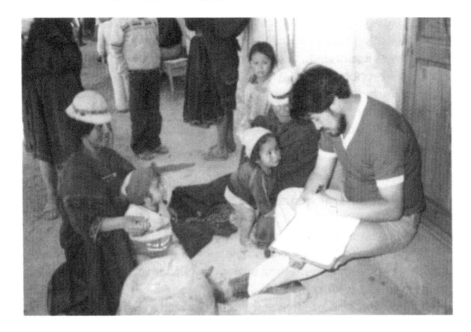

It is important for health policy makers and logistics managers to know how often their customers leave a service site disappointed because, due to a stockout, they did not receive the product they came in for. Barring medical contraindications or other unusual constraints, no informed, motivated customer should ever leave empty-handed.

countries, but no standard guidance or set of calculations specific to logistics health systems in developing countries has yet been developed (Family Planning Logistics Management, 1997a, 1997b, 1998, 2000).

Bringing it Together: Policy Makers' Role in Moving the Supply Chain from As-is to Could-be

Policy makers are expected to define and communicate the supply chain strategy – how the supply chain supports the larger organization's mission. You define who is served by the supply chain (intermediate and ultimate customers) and who participates in the supply chain (logistics system employees, contractors, suppliers, and transport personnel). You determine what information to collect and share throughout the supply chain and how to organize planning and decision-making.

Finally, you should base logistics improvement plans on accurate cost data. Only when an organization understands the economics of its entire supply chain – from manufacturer to final customer – can it monitor and improve supply chain performance.

Investing in functional improvements in supply chain operations will provide long-term payoffs in customer service, cost-effectiveness, and sustainability – these measures of your organization's progress are what really matter.

Practical Tips for Transforming the Supply Chain

As the policy level becomes more aware of how a *could-be* logistics system would benefit programmes, senior managers with responsibility for the supply chain will need to transform their operations. This involves leadership, and clarification and prioritization of specific objectives. It may also include oversight of a myriad of large and small interventions – from redesigning an LMIS form, to reroofing a warehouse, to retraining thousands of staff, to revising long-standing procurement standards.

We suggest that programme managers:

• assess the *as-is* state of supply chain operations using a comprehensive set of guidelines that includes all components and levels of the system;
• develop and implement action plans to address gaps between as-is and could-be performance;
• select and use appropriate performance measures, consistent with your system's specific objectives (for example, customer service and cost-effectiveness).

Chapter 9

Global Trends Affecting Public Sector Supply Chain Management

In Brief

Global trends in the health sector are affecting family planning and health service customers, and the practice of contraceptive and drug supply management. Policy makers and senior programme managers need to pay close attention to the trends presented in this chapter, which include management and policy issues they are likely to face in the near future. The global trends vary from country to country, but they probably affect all public health supply chains in developing countries. Supply chain managers have little or no control over most of the trends; however, they can anticipate some of the required changes and act now to adapt their supply operations.

Overall, health and family planning supply chains will be challenged during the next decade. Managers will be forced to cope with larger issues, such as integrating vertical programmes and decentralizing, while simultaneously trying to improve the effectiveness and efficiency of logistics operations to meet the demands of a growing number of customers. The global trends highlighted in this chapter will not change the mission of the supply chain – to provide a dependable supply of essential health products to customers – but the trends will change the way logistics is organized and practised. A creative response to these trends, especially at the policy level, will substantially improve supply chains and customer service.

Integrating Family Planning and Health Service Delivery

Well-integrated service delivery can reduce the duplication, waste, and lack of coordination often seen when there are many vertical programmes. However,

> Most countries implementing integrated supply chains should expect to have a blended system, not full integration.

policy makers are concerned that, without specially designated funds, impact may decline for some high-priority programmes, such as family planning. Large, vertical family planning programmes are credited with accomplishing most of the fertility decline in recent decades, yet from the mid-1990s, the long-standing debate over integrated versus vertical programmes once again favours integrated service delivery.

At the 1994 Cairo International Conference on Population and Development (ICPD), the participants endorsed an integrated reproductive health strategy (ICPD, 1994). The ICPD's Programme of Action radically departs from past thinking and redirects the international population community away from a focus on demographic changes, instead, placing the individual at the centre of all activities. Under ICPD's recommendations, a typical health reform programme delivers preventive and primary care to control communicable and non-communicable diseases, promotes and maintains reproductive health throughout life, and provides early detection and management of reproductive health problems. Services are integrated, with different types of care available at different health system levels (Merrick, 1998).

The trend toward integrated service delivery is part of a larger, global health reform movement supported by the World Bank and other international donors. Because they hope integration may improve cost-effectiveness and offer better service to clients, many developing countries are integrating or reintegrating their reproductive and primary health services, or have already done so. To date, there is very little research documenting whether the approach improves services or reduces costs, but integration is a definite feature of the health policy landscape (Mayhew, 1996; Lush et al., 1999).

Integrated service delivery may lead logically, but not necessarily, to integrated supply chains because integration is a philosophy as much as a strategy and, once accepted, is likely to influence the entire health sector, including logistics. The same rationale used to justify the shift to integrated service delivery – cost-effectiveness and better service to customers – applies equally to the supply chains providing contraceptives, vaccines, pharmaceuticals, and other health products. An integrated logistics system, for example, is potentially more effective and efficient. Supporters of integration argue that vertical supply chains function well with plentiful donor support, but are unsustainable without it. On the other hand, integrated supply chains are also more complex and difficult to manage and, therefore, potentially less reliable than vertical supply chains focused only on contraceptives.

Integration of vertical supply chains can have a political advantage for family planning because most policy makers (and politicians) care more about pharmaceuticals than contraceptives. Furthermore, family planning products (contraceptives) may be controversial, but health products (pharmaceuticals) are not. Therefore, it could be advantageous to family planning if contraceptives were to become part of a fully supported, integrated supply chain where contraceptive procurement and distribution are politically better protected. Conversely, because contraceptives are often valued less than pharmaceuticals, some managers fear that contraceptives will be neglected or forgotten in an integrated supply chain. These arguments and counter-arguments should be evaluated for each specific programme and country.

Supply chains can be fully integrated (all types of commodities and supplies handled together) or partially integrated (integrated for some products or functions, but separate for others). Most countries implementing integrated supply chains should expect to have a blended system, not full integration. Today, in fact, few fully integrated, public sector contraceptive and pharmaceutical logistics systems exist anywhere in the world.

Nepal has integrated its previously vertical family planning and health logistics systems. After a period of adjustment, a stronger and more efficient logistics system emerged, designed to handle all categories of essential health products. Duplication was eliminated. Donors historically supporting only health or family planning now permit their funds to be used to strengthen the integrated system in areas such as transport, training, and logistics technical assistance. Although Nepal's is an integrated system, not all products are available with the same reliability; because of the availability of donor funds for supplies, contraceptives remain more available than most other products.

To maintain the flow of contraceptives during integration, most countries integrate gradually, carefully managing the process to preserve the gains made by the former vertical contraceptive distribution system. As a rule, integrated supply chains function at an operating efficiency equal to the least efficient component of the system. Many successful contraceptive distribution systems have been pulled down to the lower operating efficiency of the pharmaceutical systems with which they were merged. For this reason, a good strategy is to improve the weaker supply chain by improving the information system, distribution practices, and customer focus first, before beginning the integration process. It is a mistake to believe that, with integration, the stronger supply chain improves the weaker one. More likely, the opposite happens.

With widely varying results, many countries are already merging their contraceptive and pharmaceutical supply chains – including Bangladesh,

In a blended system, integration means the supply chain is integrated for some products or functions, but separate for others – whatever makes the most sense to guarantee the availability of priority products to customers. Transport is one of the simplest logistics functions to integrate.

Malawi, Mali, Nepal, the Philippines, Tanzania, and Zambia. To date, logistics management information systems (LMIS) have been the most adversely affected by integration. In some cases, the LMIS has either been abolished or altered, so accurate and timely information on the quantities of contraceptives dispensed to users is no longer routinely available to guide forecasting and distribution decisions.

Contraceptive supply chain managers shifting into integrated systems will find pharmaceutical logistics more complex than contraceptive logistics, because:

- many more products must be managed;
- there is a wider range of products and storage requirements;
- more rationing decisions must be made because demand for drugs almost always exceeds supply, partially due to far less donor funding for drug procurement than for contraceptives;

Integrating contraceptives and other products into one supply chain is possible, but it requires careful planning. Some pharmaceuticals, such as these vaccines being unloaded in cold boxes, require special storage and handling.

- more procurement options are available because of the many drug manufacturers and suppliers, both local and international;
- new logistics issues must be dealt with, such as cost recovery and revolving drug funds, drug selection according to therapeutic value, and efficient dispensing practices.

Integrated health and family planning logistics systems require more sophisticated supply chain management; highly qualified personnel with special skills; and complex, automated information systems. To function effectively, the systems also require additional policy-level oversight and support.

Logistics systems and product availability have been a powerful factor in many successful vertical public health efforts, from global disease eradication to national family planning service delivery programmes (Fenner et al., 1988). It is of overriding importance, when the possibility of integration is first discussed by policy makers, that logistics be included. In these strategic discussions, 'logistics' should be understood to comprise both supply chain operations and a commitment to product availability. The earlier in the integration process the logistics system is planned, the more likely it is that the programmes will succeed.

Without good planning, integration can create serious problems. One African country had a well-functioning contraceptive distribution system, supported by an effective LMIS. As part of decentralization, the government decided to integrate contraceptives into the essential drug supply system, treating them like any other essential drug – charging a fee to clients and using the drug management record keeping system. With that change, the contraceptive LMIS suddenly ceased to exist, and the numerous staff trained to use the system were no longer needed. At the same time, the supervisory system no longer functioned, and provisions were not made for supervision of the newly integrated system. Better planning could have eliminated many of the subsequent problems.

Guinea is taking a gradual approach to integration. Policy makers at the MOH agreed to have an integrated system. At present, however, neither of the logistics systems to be integrated works satisfactorily. The officials understand the need to make long-term decisions about the products, processes (for example, transport, storage, LMIS, and training), and levels to include in the pipeline (central, regional, district, and service delivery points). Everyone agrees that the criteria for integration are efficiency, coverage, and cost savings.

Decentralizing Health Service Management

Decentralization, which pushes responsibility for health services management down to intermediate and lower levels, is a key strategy of the current health reform movement (Cassels, 1995). Closely linked to integration, decentralization encourages policy makers to replace highly centralized, vertical services with decentralized, integrated services. The rationale for decentralization is that local managers can make more effective and efficient resource allocation decisions than distant, central-level officials. However, decentralization can multiply, rather than correct, problems of mismanagement.

The trend in modern logistics management is to increase effectiveness and efficiency by consolidating the LMIS, procurement, and distribution management at higher levels – the exact opposite of decentralization. It is a strategic decision for commercial supply chains to centralize information

> The trend in modern logistics management is to increase effectiveness and efficiency by consolidating the LMIS, procurement, and distribution management at higher levels – the exact opposite of decentralization.

management and decision-making, which provides the most control over the logistics system, keeps it focused on its core purpose, and makes it more responsive to customers. But, MOHs usually decentralize for political, not supply chain-related, reasons. Inevitably, they move decision-making to lower levels and downsize the logistics management staff at the central level. Supply chain performance often suffers.

One potentially negative aspect of decentralization is that procurement works best for larger volumes. Bulk purchasing is more cost-effective because unit costs decrease with volume. If decentralization causes procurement budgets, decisions, and processes to shift to the lower levels, the actual availability of essential supplies like contraceptives may be jeopardized, or costs may rise.

Every detail and routine aspect of logistics operations is affected by health reforms, such as integration, decentralization, and cost recovery.

LMISs, often designed to channel data quickly to the central level for decision-making, are usually disrupted (and can collapse) during decentralization. Information systems require a major redesign to operate effectively in a decentralized environment. Retraining is required throughout the supply chain to prepare personnel responsible for contraceptive availability within a decentralized system.

Assuming procurement and information systems remain centralized, decentralization of other logistics management responsibilities may have positive effects:

- logistics decisions are made closer to customers and can result in improved customer service;
- redesigned LMISs bring automation and improved data to lower levels of the supply chain;
- technical logistics skills are practised by more personnel at more levels, potentially making a decentralized supply chain more resilient and less vulnerable to disruption.

As an example, Chile's efforts to decentralize have kept the family planning logistics programme strong. Chile's strongly centralized government has decentralized health budgets to the regional level. With midwives serving as regional health managers for both family planning and primary health care programmes, support for family planning remains intact, and the national budget has a specific line item for contraceptives. Although responsibility for the health budgets was decentralized, the central-level health administration carries out the national procurement of commodities.

In one African country, however, decentralizing the logistics system had negative effects. Different parts of the country are supported by different donors, and the groups do little information sharing. It is hard to get data on stock levels and consumption rates. Forecasting at the national level is difficult, and stockouts are common.

In one Latin American country, contraceptive supply may be in jeopardy because of some aspects of decentralization. The central MOH procures contraceptives (to take advantage of economies of scale), but the regions are in charge of their procurement budgets, product selection, and forecasting.

> Successful outsourcing requires strong skills in negotiating and managing contracts.

Since these responsibilities were devolved to the regions, there has been a striking 75 per cent decline in the procurement of oral contraceptives by the central level. Supporters of family planning are increasingly concerned that the autonomous regional health administrations, usually headed by medical doctors, may be giving less attention to procuring contraceptives in favour of other commodities and programmes. Will the decentralization of budgetary decision-making mean not enough contraceptives are procured by the central level on behalf of the regions?

Increasing Private Sector Involvement in Health

In the 1980s, a global movement emerged that applied private sector approaches to public sector services and enhanced the role of the private sector, including NGOs, in providing health care in developing countries. The private sector was seen as flexible and innovative, and competition was thought to produce efficient allocation of health resources. This movement continues today. However, it is now accepted that the private sector is not automatically more flexible, innovative, or efficient, and, more important, that the private sector has no mandate to serve the whole population (including poor or remote subpopulations), as the public sector does. So the role of the public sector remains vital.

Advocates of increased private sector involvement strongly influenced the development of health policy in the 1990s. The World Bank and other international donors support the growing private sector involvement in health, and this trend is likely to continue (World Bank, 1993). The trend encompasses:

- a greater role for private or nongovernmental providers of services;
- outsourcing key functions to private sector companies;
- wholly privatizing some operations.

Public sector services are shrinking in most developing countries. Stagnant or declining government health budgets frequently lower the quality of government-sponsored health services. Low pay and loss of status increasingly demoralize government health workers, and government facilities are chronically short of supplies and equipment. Partly in response to this decline, the private sector (including NGOs) is assuming a larger health care role in many countries.

An efficient logistics system improves the cost-effectiveness of health services.

The expanding role of NGOs in reproductive health care will probably require major modifications in the organization and management of public sector contraceptive supply chains. Governments and donors have traditionally supplied NGOs with contraceptives, but, in most countries, the quantities were small compared with the overall national consumption. However, as NGOs expand reproductive health services, their contraceptive requirements will increase, placing a new demand on supply chains designed to cater to the public sector. Contraceptive forecasting must now consider NGO requirements. LMISs should be adapted to fit the needs of NGOs, and distribution networks will need to accommodate the growing contraceptive consumption at NGO service centres.

In addition to new and expanded roles for private sector providers of health services, the private sector is increasingly involved in other aspects of health service management in developing countries. For example, public sector logistics systems now often contract with private companies for supply functions, such as port clearance, warehousing, and transport. The starting point for such outsourcing is often contracting private carriers to deliver contraceptives. Successful outsourcing requires specialized skills not traditionally found in public sector supply chains – the ability to determine the feasibility of contracting; drawing up, negotiating, and interpreting contracts; and monitoring contractor performance and negotiating differences.

Most public sector supply chain managers spend their careers in government, and, consequently, need to increase their understanding of how to conduct business with the private sector. Individuals need to develop new skills; institutions – ministries – need to improve their management systems. For example, the public sector needs to develop more efficient payment mechanisms and punctual, disciplined logistics operations able to interface smoothly with private contractors. Experience shows that governments' timely payment of contractors' invoices is of critical importance. Their failure to pay promptly can rupture the supply chain.

Privatization, in contrast to outsourcing, means that portions of the supply chain pass from government to private control. Privatization, which varies greatly from country to country, is becoming more common in pharmaceutical management, where some government medical stores are being converted into autonomous parastatal organizations governed by commercial principles. Governments continue to formulate drug policies, and government representatives usually sit on the boards of directors of the new autonomous entities, but day-to-day operations are managed like commercial companies.

Privatization of a central medical store requires major changes – legal, administrative, and political – at the central level, but comparatively little restructuring at the lower levels. Managers of privatized supply chains are far more cost conscious than managers of the public sector systems they replace, and, consequently, LMISs often need to be revised to collect and report more financial data. More favourable terms of employment in a privatized system, combined with a new senior management team, usually improve morale and performance. With appropriate planning and oversight, a privatized supply chain, more oriented toward customer service, should mean improved contraceptive availability throughout the distribution network.

Emphasizing Cost-effectiveness

In recent years, as health costs have risen rapidly while government spending on health has levelled off or declined, government health services in developing countries have come under increasing scrutiny from economists and financial analysts. To stretch dwindling resources, governments and donors now look for ways to improve the cost-effectiveness of health services (Hill, 1998). Logistics is a high-leverage function, meaning that small changes in logistics processes can result in big changes in inventory, transportation, customer satisfaction, and cost-effectiveness (Marien, 1999).

Cost-effectiveness is increasingly a criterion by which scarce health resources are allocated, yet the actual costs of operating supply chains in developing countries – vertical or integrated – are not well documented. To begin the process of improving cost-effectiveness, supply chain managers must identify all the costs associated with their systems. In the late 1990s, the need to quantify the value of logistics received a lot of attention in the commercial sector. Techniques now exist for costing out the supply chain and relating those costs to the performance of the organization; such exercises should be undertaken in the public health sector to demonstrate the value of the logistics function (Keebler et al., 1999).

Cost-effectiveness arguments usually drive the merger of contraceptive and pharmaceutical supply chains. Therefore, senior managers need to understand thoroughly cost-effectiveness methodology, its terminology and, especially,

Potential cost savings from improving drug logistics are significant: 25 per cent savings by using proper storage, 15 per cent with proper inventory control that reduces expiry, and 20 per cent by reducing theft and pilferage (Foster, 1991). For contraceptives, the potential savings may be somewhat lower than the figures for drugs, but the savings are still significant. One example from Kenya is quite dramatic: costly sexually transmitted infection (STI) treatment kits were 'stretched' by more than 400 per cent using proper distribution, based on consumption data (supplying more than 500 sites for two years, not the 143 sites for one year envisioned in the original plan). If the kits had been distributed to the pilot programme sites on the schedule envisioned at the time of donor procurement, a large volume of supplies would have been wasted, and the numerous new service sites added to the programme would have gone empty-handed needlessly (Regional Centre for Quality of Health Care, 1999b).

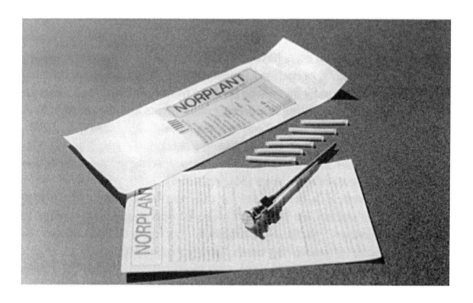

Charging fees to recover costs may affect utilization. In Malawi, in 1997, with the government-supported health facilities charging US$5.50 for Norplant® insertions, there were about five customers a month. After the fee was waived, the number of insertions increased to about 45 a month. Cost-related fluctuations in demand create uncertainty in the supply chain.

how to make sound decisions about the supply chain, based on cost-study findings. Future LMISs will need to collect and report more cost data to managers and policy makers. Cost criteria are likely to be used increasingly in supply chain design and operational decisions, and cost consciousness will permeate the public health supply chain in a way not seen in the past.

Introducing Cost Recovery

Cost recovery, another cost-related trend, is a major reform initiative that encourages people to invest in their own health. The most common cost-recovery mechanism is charging user fees to cover some of the recurrent costs of health service. Cost recovery seems to work best for curative services, although studies show that the recovery rate from user fees is only about 5 per cent of the total recurrent government expenditures (Berman, 1995). Governments, NGOs, and donors have traditionally subsidized preventive services, such as family planning, but pressure is growing for clients to contribute more to the cost of these services.

Cost recovery will affect supply chains in at least these four ways:

1   as distribution and other programme costs rise, pressure will increase for customers to pay part of the increased costs;
2   when client fees are raised as part of cost recovery, contraceptive consumption often drops suddenly and may be erratic for many months, resulting in stock imbalances;
3   well-controlled, accountable systems must be designed to handle cash and financial data, and logistics and service delivery staff will need additional skills to manage funds;
4   the mission-critical importance of logistics rises dramatically after cost recovery is introduced, and the service delivery environment becomes more of a retail environment. Simply put, you cannot sell what you do not have on your shelves. To maximize the potential of a cost recovery programme, the supply chain must be especially effective and responsive.

Serving the Growing Numbers of Family Planning Users

While the rate of world population growth is slowing, generally the highest

> To maximize cost-recovery, the supply chain must be especially effective.

rate of population growth is occurring in poor regions where people depend on public sector family planning programmes. Global contraceptive prevalence is estimated at approximately 56 per cent, but this average masks a range from less than 5 per cent to more than 70 per cent. In different countries, worldwide, 120 million to 150 million women still have unmet needs for family planning (White, 1998). The number of family planning users is likely to grow rapidly in the coming decade.

This growth in new family planning users has several implications for the supply chain. Logistics systems will experience an increase in the volume of products handled, and distribution networks will expand to serve more and more customers. Both of these factors mean increased workloads for the logistics system. Supply chains serving areas with low contraceptive prevalence (below 30 per cent) can expect large increases in the number of contraceptives moving through the distribution network – the result of many new customers. Costs of operating the expanding supply chain – storage, distribution, training, and data processing – will rise, bringing pressure for more efficient operations, including streamlining existing distribution networks and providing extensive automation.

Expanding the Variety of Contraceptives

New types of contraceptives are being introduced – the female condom and the one-month injectable are two of the newest methods available. High-quality family planning programmes emphasize informed choice, which means giving customers a choice of methods and brands. Social marketing programmes are segmenting their markets and introducing brands aimed at each one. In the coming decade, these trends indicate a continuing increase in the number of contraceptive products, which means a more complex supply chain.

Ordering, receiving, storing, and distributing a larger number of items means additional handling and distribution costs, increasing overall supply chain costs. Sophisticated supply chain management will be needed to handle the greater variety of items, especially in forecasting, inventory management, and distribution. Every additional item will challenge the supply chain to operate at a higher level of efficiency just to maintain the same level of contraceptive availability for customers.

Burden of disease data may influence policy makers to expand reproductive health and family planning programmes, increasing the volume of contraceptives handled by these supply chains.

Rising Customer Expectations

Rising customer expectations is a worldwide phenomenon that affects the marketing of all products, including contraceptives. Family planning users expect an increasingly higher standard of service from the service delivery programme and, consequently, from the logistics system: increased variety of items, consistent quality, and convenient availability.

Customer service has become the guiding principle of state-of-the-art supply chain operations. Public sector supply chains without a history of customer orientation will need to catch up. Customer satisfaction will need to be measured, either in special surveys or as part of the LMIS, to allow individual and overall system performance monitoring and improvement. Interpersonal skills of frontline staff must be improved so the staff can relate better to customers, and customer-friendly attitudes will need to be instilled throughout the supply chain so intermediate customers – warehouses, stores, and service delivery points – are well stocked to provide service to the ultimate customer. The slogan, No customer should ever leave a clinic disappointed because the product he or she needs is out of stock, evokes the customer service mentality and highlights how important it is for the logistics system to deliver the products people want.

Rising Policy Maker Expectations

Logistics has moved from the 'back room to the boardroom' in the commercial sector, and the same trend is occurring in the public sector (Hart, 1995). As a result, logistics is assuming a higher profile in family planning and health organizations as policy makers increasingly recognize logistics as a key function. More resources and attention are being given to the supply chain by governments and donors, and a higher level of performance is expected (Martin, 1997).

Contraceptive supply chains will come under closer scrutiny; shortfalls and other supply problems are more likely to be noticed by policy makers.

To work productively with colleagues at the policy level, senior supply chain managers will need academic and professional qualifications (LeMay and Carr, 1999). Supply chain staff will be expected to operate at higher levels of effectiveness and efficiency, requiring additional training to improve their technical skills and competence. Policy makers will probably expect increased reporting of supply chain performance to the policy level, including cost-effectiveness data, which means more systematic and regular monitoring of supply functions and their costs.

Using the Burden of Disease Approach

Christopher Murray and his colleagues at Harvard University developed a revolutionary approach for measuring health status, quantifying the number of deaths and the impact of premature death and disability, and combining them into a single unit of measurement called the 'burden of disease' (Murray and Lopez, 1996). With the endorsement of the World Bank and the World Health Organization, this new approach is growing in importance as a tool for measuring health status and influencing health policy. The burden of disease approach clearly highlights the loss of life and health caused by unsafe sex. For example, unsafe sex – including both infections and the complications of unwanted pregnancy – is responsible for 2.2 per cent of total global deaths. In young adult women in sub-Saharan Africa, unsafe sex accounts for almost one-third of the total disease burden. These data strongly suggest that countries will or should be increasing their investment in reproductive health.

If burden of disease data influence policy makers to expand reproductive health and family planning programmes, the volume of contraceptives and other primary health commodities handled by the supply chain will increase. Senior managers need to understand the burden of disease approach so they can interpret data and anticipate its impact on logistics operations, especially forecasting, procurement, and LMIS.

With multiple donors, coordinating forecasting, procurement, and reporting requirements becomes increasingly complex.

Increasing Number of Contraceptive Donors

In the past, it was common for a country to have one major contraceptive donor, but today countries are likely to have at least two or three. The British Department for International Development (DFID), the German funding agency for international development (KfW), and the European Union have joined USAID and the United Nations Population Fund (UNFPA) to supply significant quantities of contraceptives to developing countries. In addition, countries increasingly use World Bank funds to support their commodity requirements. Because of growing needs, more contraceptive donors are likely to become involved. The estimate for the cost of contraceptive requirements for 1997 alone was US$818 million. This figure will probably be well over US$1 billion per year by 2010 (United Nations Population Fund, n.d.).

With multiple donors and lenders involved, coordinating forecasting, procurement, and reporting requirements becomes increasingly complex. Supply chain managers' organizational and communication skills are needed to coordinate the various parties. LMISs must become more sophisticated and preferably computerized. Forecasts need to be updated more frequently and the pipeline monitored more closely, because less agile donors require a longer lead time and are less able to respond to shortages with emergency shipments. With multiple supply sources, more attention must be given to quality issues. These changes will require training and retraining to improve the performance of logistics personnel; procurement and data management costs are also likely to increase significantly.

Incorporating New Technologies

As we have noted many times, information technology – computers – and modern logistics are closely linked. To realize significant improvements in efficiency, logistics practitioners in health supply chains in developing countries need to keep pace with the trends in information technology. Web-based procurement processes and logistics training via the Internet are within reach. Cutting-edge advances in bar coding, hand-held radio-frequency scanners, electronic picking systems, and sophisticated warehouse locator systems may not be needed yet by many health supply chains, but many central medical stores and central warehouses could use these technologies immediately. Other new equipment may be warranted as well: energy-efficient forklifts, pallet-racking systems, and versatile shelving.

As in many fields, however, logistics is said to be only 20 per cent technology and 80 per cent people. The attraction of new technology should not be for itself, but for what people can accomplish with it. To take advantage of technological advances, people must have the proper skills. Today, the most highly desired abilities for logisticians include computer literacy, financial management capability, and effective communications skills (LeMay and Carr 1999). New technologies can improve and enhance the workplace, but the main focus should still be on people.

Streamlining Distribution Networks

The trend in commercial logistics is for distribution networks to have fewer levels, leading to faster delivery to customers at reduced costs. In developed countries, computerization of the LMIS and improved transportation infrastructures made this streamlining possible.

A major stumbling block to streamlining distribution networks in the public sector is that many supply chains simply mirror government administrative structures; decentralization can actually work against the trend toward streamlined distribution. Nevertheless, future contraceptive supply chains should have fewer rather than more levels. Supply chains increasingly need to delink from government administrative structures, because having fewer levels reduces overall costs – less money goes to inventory and intermediate warehouses and stores (but more goes to transportation).

To keep a shorter pipeline filled, both donor and local procurement must be more responsive. A distribution network with fewer levels must operate efficiently, because fewer intermediate levels (with safety stocks as a cushion against logistics mistakes) stand between the supplier and customer.

Increasing Demand for Condoms Due to HIV/AIDS and STI

Worldwide, more than 30 million people are infected with the HIV virus, and it continues to spread – one estimate states that 21 million people in

> For a commodity phaseover to succeed, the financial resources, technical skill, and management systems must be there; and powerful people need to care about the availability of supplies.

sub-Saharan Africa are infected (Bloom, 1998). Condoms are an effective preventive weapon against HIV; consequently, the demand for condoms as STI/HIV protection is rising, often dramatically, in countries with high HIV prevalence.

As vertical HIV/AIDS prevention activities integrate into reproductive health services, the practice of separately managing condoms for HIV prevention is declining. Logistics systems originally established to supply contraceptives for family planning will now handle an increasing number of condoms to control HIV, which has implications for every supply chain function. Because condoms are bulky items and are required in large volumes, they pose special challenges for storage and transport – especially at the end of the supply chain, the service delivery point, where the 'storage facility' may literally be a cabinet and the 'transport link' may be a bicycle. Even one large carton of condoms quickly strains capacity. To support HIV activities, supply chains may need to establish customized condom delivery networks to handle this bulk and volume and to reach non-family planning service sites and distribution points. LMISs may need to be revised to capture and report information on condoms dispensed from new, non-traditional outlets and to new, non-family planning users. Condom forecasts should include all potential consumption and consider projected increases in HIV prevalence.

Phasing Over Contraceptive Procurement

Some countries and programmes that traditionally received donated products and donor-funded logistics system support are now sufficiently mature to assume gradual or complete fiscal and managerial responsibility for contraceptive procurement. This transfer or phaseover of responsibilities is sometimes called achieving self-reliance, or graduation, for contraceptives and logistics. Several countries (for example, Chile, Colombia, Thailand, Costa Rica, Botswana, and Tunisia) completed this process successfully. Other countries (for example, Morocco and Turkey) are completing the process now. Still other countries, such as Zimbabwe and Indonesia, started or even completed the process and then encountered serious difficulties or setbacks, usually from macroeconomic causes.

In countries completing this transition, the process has not been evaluated sufficiently to accurately determine exactly what works and what does not. However, some broad factors appear to be critical to a successful phaseover, the most important being adequate resources, political will, technical capability, and sufficiently strong administrative and managerial structures to ensure continued availability of supplies to the end user (Hutchings and Hart, 1994). The phaseover process typically takes 5–10 years and is the result of thorough and iterative planning among host country organizations, donors, and technical assistance partners. For a commodity phaseover to succeed, the financial resources, technical skill, and management systems must be there; and people – powerful people at the top – need to care about the availability of supplies. The trend toward phasing over mature programmes requires closer scrutiny to ensure that they can succeed without donated products or donor-funded logistics assistance.

Ensuring Contraceptive Security

Given the rising need for contraceptives in developing countries and the uncertainty of global financing for continuous full supply, the issue of contraceptive security is beginning to receive attention. Like food security in famine-prone locations, contraceptive security begins with knowing your risks and taking steps to ensure the adequacy of future supplies. To what extent have country programmes identified their contraceptive requirements for the medium- or long-term future? When budgeting and procurement cycles span multiple years, and in-country pipelines can be 24 months long, knowing there are enough supplies in the pipeline for next year's needs is not security. To what extent have country programmes and donors committed resources to support supply needs? The resource allocation process within government and donor bureaucracies is time-consuming, complicated, and typically underestimated as an obstacle. To what extent do in-country distribution systems reliably supply contraceptives to service providers and, ultimately, to end users? Real security means that supplies reliably reach the ultimate customers.

Contraceptive security exists when programmes:

- accurately estimate their requirements; and
- either have or coordinate the resources needed to meet them for the medium-term future (5–10 years); and
- effectively move those supplies to end users.

To advance any health agenda, the availability of essential supplies must be ensured. Products must be made available from donors or national governments to their priority programmes, and they must be made available by these programmes to their clients. The notion of commodity security is vital for any health programme to which a country is politically committed, yet the question of the adequacy and security of supplies is often not addressed at the policy level. Supply chain functions – from procurement to transport to LMIS, and from donor coordination to customer service – are critical elements of contraceptive security.

Bringing It Together

The supply chain does not operate in isolation from the larger health service organization. Logistics' mission is to enable programme success, but it can only do so when it receives adequate resources and strong policy support. Political, economic, and social trends challenge the supply chain for contraceptives and essential health commodities in developing countries. Skilful planning and the inclusion of supply chain considerations at the policy level allow logistics systems to be an important part of the solution for public health problems.

The supply chain links programmes to customers.

> Remember, logistics helps programmes deliver!

Practical Tips for Responding to Global Trends

How can policy makers and programme managers anticipate and respond to global trends that affect the supply chain? At least part of the answer lies in taking 'the 10,000 meter view' – flying over the landscape gives a new perspective to things that are happening on the ground. Sometimes, to be most practical and effective, leaders and managers need to escape from their day-to-day concerns and contemplate the bigger issues.

• Keep abreast of current developments in the field of logistics. Participate in local or regional business and professional associations that focus on supply chain management; they exist on every continent. If there are no affiliations in your area, read business and logistics trade publications or use the Internet. Begin with the Family Planning Logistics Management project (www.fplm.jsi.com), the Council of Logistics Management (www.clm1.org) or the Supply-Chain Council (www.supply-chain.org), and follow the links from there.
• Stay alert to local and national political and administrative changes. Do not let the logistics system be an after-thought during government reorganization, decentralization, devolution, and downsizing – keep the supply chain on the agenda.
• Continually upgrade the skills of both senior managers and logistics staff, especially in business and financial management, information technology, and communications. Ideally, programmes encourage trained staff to lead the way, instead of training staff to catch up to events.
• Spread the supply chain perspective on commodity availability and longer-term commodity security as a mission-critical aspect of all health programmes. When planning new HIV activities or introducing essential services packages, or anticipating graduation from donor dependence, ask the question, 'How will this programme guarantee that essential supplies are reliably and continuously available to all customers?'
• Design and operate sound, responsive logistics systems (consistent with the principles in chapters 1–3 and the practices in chapters 4–8). Most importantly, keep flexibility and expandability in mind. Systems cannot be so rigid that things like introducing new products or adding new distribution outlets pose major obstacles.

- Be open to new ways of doing business – outsourcing or privatizing some functions, eliminating levels in the system, or using new technologies – if they improve the logistics system's ability to meet its customer service objectives.
- Always remember the customer. In every discussion, strategic planning meeting, or budgeting session, return the focus to better customer service. The need to adapt your operations to address trends like the ones discussed in this chapter will not stop, but the customer service mission of the logistics system should never change.

Bibliography

Abrahamsson, Mats and Brege Staffan (1997), 'Structural Changes in the Supply Chain', *The International Journal of Logistics Management*, 8: 35–44.

Ackerman, Kenneth B. (1999), 'Designing Tomorrow's Warehouse: A Little Ahead of the Times', *Journal of Business Logistics*, 20 (1): 1–4.

Aitken, Iain W. (1999), 'Implementation and Integration of Reproductive Health Services on a Decentralized System', in Riitta-Liisa Kolehmainhen-Aitken (ed.), *Myths and Realities about the Decentralization of Health Systems*, Boston: Management Sciences for Health.

Albrecht, Karl and Ron Zemke (1990), *Service America!*, New York: Warner Books Inc.

Altabet, Robert (1998), 'The Forecaster as a Key Member of the Strategic Planning Team', *The Journal of Business Forecasting* (Fall): 3–6.

Andel, Tom (1996a), 'CEOs Share Visions of Supply Chains', *Transportation & Distribution* (May): 109–112.

Andel, Tom (1996b), 'Flow It, Don't Stow It', *Transportation & Distribution* (May): 60–64.

Andel, Tom (1997a), 'Demand Forecasting: How to Win at Educated Guessing', *Transportation & Distribution* (June): 54–59.

Andel, Tom (1997b), 'Get Your Warehouse Out of Storage', *Transportation & Distribution* (May): 94–105.

Andel, Tom (1997c), 'Going Hyper, Being Agile', *Transportation & Distribution* (November): 99.

Andel, Tom (1997d), 'Make Connections in the Chain', *Transportation & Distribution* (January): 43–52.

Andel, Tom (1997e), 'Make the World Your Warehouse', *Transportation & Distribution* (August): 88–92.

Anderson, David L. and Hau Lee (1999), 'Synchronized Supply Chains: The New Frontier', in *Achieving Supply Chain Excellence through Technology*, 12–21, San Francisco: Montgomery Research, Inc.

Anderson, Matthew G. and Paul B. Katz (1998), 'Strategic Sourcing', *The International Journal of Logistics Management*, 9 (1): 1–13.

Andraski, Joseph C. (1998), 'Leadership and the Realization of Supply Chain Collaboration', *Journal of Business Logistics*, 19 (2): 9–11.

Aron, Laurie Joan (1996), 'Food Industry Logistics: Beyond the Point of Sale', *Inbound Logistics* (August): 19–30.

Aron, Laurie Joan (1997), 'Pulling the Switch on Excess Inventory', *Inbound Logistics* (May): 48–52.

Aron, Laurie Joan (1999a), 'Logistics from the Mountaintop', *Inbound Logistics* (January): 98–106.

Aron, Laurie Joan (1999b), 'Online Learning Anytime, Anywhere', *Inbound Logistics* (February): 19–24.

Arthur D. Little Inc. and the Pennsylvania State University for The Council of Logistics Management (1991), *Logistics in Service Industries*, Oakbrook, Ill.: The Council of Logistics Management.

Ayala, Beatriz (1999), 'Supply Chain Mapping', paper, Malawi: Ministry of Health and Population, Arlington, Va.: Family Planning Logistics Management/John Snow Inc.

Ayers, Allan F. (1999), 'What Logistics Managers Need To Know about Today's Complex Information Systems', *Transportation & Distribution* (September): 33–8.

Ballou, Ronald H. (1988), *Business Logistics Management*, Upper Saddle River, NJ: Prentice Hall Inc.

Bardi, Edward J., T.S. Raghunathan and Prabir K. Bagchi (1994), 'Logistics Information Systems: The Strategic Role of Top Management', *Journal of Business Logistics*, 15 (1): 71–85.

Bartholomew, Doug (1998), 'IT delivers for UPS', *Industry Week*, 237 (23): 58–64.

Bates, James A., Ramona Lunt, Jennifer Crandall, Richard C. Owens Jr, Tony Hudgins and Gary Steele (1998), *Family Planning Logistics Management (FPLM) Orientation to Essential Drug Supply Management*, Arlington, Va.: Family Planning Logistics Management/John Snow Inc.

Bechtel, Christian and Jayanth Jayaram (1997), 'Supply Chain Management: A Strategic Perspective', *The International Journal of Logistics Management*, 8 (1): 15–34.

Berman, Peter (1995), *Health Sector Reform in Developing Countries: Making Health Development Sustainable*, Harvard Series on Population and International Health, Cambridge, Mass.: Harvard University Press.

Bertrand, Jane T., Robert J. Magnani and James C. Knowles (1994), *Handbook of Indicators for Family Planning Program Evaluation*, Chapel Hill, NC: The Evaluation Project, Carolina Population Center, University of North Carolina at Chapel Hill.

Birou, Laura M. and Stanley E. Fawcett (1993), 'International Purchasing: Benefits, Requirements and Challenges', *International Journal of Purchasing and Materials Management*, 29 (2): 27–37.

Bloom, David (1998), *The Burden of Disease in Africa*, Cambridge, Mass.: Harvard Institute for International Development.

Bovet, David M. and Bob W. Martin (1998), 'Achieving Strategic Transportation Effectiveness', *Logistics!* (Winter/Spring): 2–17.

Bovet, David M. and Yossi Sheffi (1998), 'The Brave New World of Supply Chain Management', *Supply Chain Management Review*, 14–22.

Bowman, Robert J. (1998), 'Build a Solid Future: 10 Steps to Material Handling Success!', *Warehousing Management* (March): 14–18.

Braithwaite, Alan W. and Martin Christopher (1991), 'Managing the Global Pipeline', *The International Journal of Logistics Management*, 2: 55–62.

Braithwaite, Alan W. and Paul J. Howard (1993), 'Logistics Systems or Customer Focused Organization: Which Comes First?', paper presented at Council of Logistics Management Annual Conference, Washington, DC, 3–6 October.

Brewer, Peter C. and Thomas W. Speh (2000), 'Using the Balance Scorecard to Measure Supply Chain Performance', *Journal of Business Logistics*, 21 (1).

Bruce, Judith (1990), 'Fundamental Elements of Quality of Care: A Simple Framework', *Studies in Family Planning*, 21 (2): 61–91.

Bulatao, Rodolfo A. (1995), 'Key Indicators for Family Planning Projects', World Bank Technical Paper, no. 297, Washington: World Bank.

Burgess, Rachel (1998), 'Avoiding Supply Chain Management Failure: Lessons from Business Process Reengineering', *The International Journal of Logistics Management*, 9: 15–23.

Carlsson, Jan and Hans Sarv (1997), 'Mastering Logistics Change', *The International Journal of Logistics Management*, 8: 45–54.

Cassels, Andrew (1995), 'Health Sector Reform: Key Issues in Less Developed Countries', Discussion paper 1, Geneva: Division of Strengthening Health Services, World Health Organization.

Chambers, John C., Satinda K. Mullick and Donald D. Smith (1971), 'How to Choose the Right Forecasting Technique', *Harvard Business Review* (July–August): 45–74.

Chi, Keon S. (1999), 'Improving Responsiveness', *Public Administration Review*, 59 (May/June): 278–80.

Christopher, Martin (1986), *The Strategy of Distribution Management*, Westport, Conn.: Quorum Books.

Christopher, Martin (1999), 'Creating the Agile Supply Chain', in *Achieving Supply Chain Excellence through Technology*, 28–32, San Francisco: Montgomery Research, Inc.

Closs, David J. (1989), 'Inventory Management: A Comparison of Traditional vs. Systems View', *Journal of Business Logistics*, 10 (2): 90–105.

Cooper, Martha C., Douglas M. Lambert and Janus D. Pagh (1997), 'Supply Chain Management: More Than a New Name for Logistics', *The International Journal of Logistics Management*, 8 (1): 1–14.

Copacino, William C. (1997), *Supply Chain Management: The Basics and Beyond*, Boca Raton, Fla.: St Lucie Press.

Copacino, William C. (1998), 'The Barriers to Supply-chain Excellence', *Logistics Management* (March): 39.

Cox, Andrew (1998), 'Clarifying Complexity', *Supply Management* (January 29): 34–36.

Coyle, J.J., Edward J. Bardi and Joseph L. Cavinato (1990), *Transportation*, St Paul, Minn.: West Publishing Company.

'Customer Service – Walking the Walk' (1996), *Inbound Logistics* (December): 21–27.

Dadzie, Kofie Q. (1998), 'Transfer of Logistics Knowledge to Third World Countries', *International Journal of Physical Distribution and Logistics*, 28 (4): 272–83.

Davis, Frank W. and Brian J. Gibson (1993), 'Service Response Logistics: Rethinking the Concept of Logistics', paper presented at the Council of Logistics Management Annual Conference, Washington, DC, 3–6 October.

Davis, Tom (1993), 'Effective Supply Chain Management', *Sloan Management Review*: 35–46.

Dobler, Donald W. and David N. Burt (1996), *Purchasing and Supply Management*, New York: McGraw-Hill.

Dresner, Martin and Kefeng Xu (1995), 'Customer Service, Customer Satisfaction and Corporate Performance in the Service Sector', *Journal of Business Logistics*, 16: 23–40.

Family Planning Logistics Management (FPLM) (1994), *Family Planning and MCH Logistics in Bangladesh: An Overview*, Arlington, Va.: FPLM/John Snow Inc.

Family Planning Logistics Management (1995a), *Composite Indicators for Contraceptive Logistics Management*, Arlington, Va.: FPLM/John Snow Inc.

Family Planning Logistics Management (1995b), *The Forecasting Cookbook: A Commodity Forecasting and Requirements Estimation Manual for Family Planning and AIDS/STD Prevention Programs*, Arlington, Va.: FPLM /John Snow Inc.

Family Planning Logistics Management (1997a), *A Strategic Approach to the Rationalization of Distribution under the Integrated Population and Health Program*, Arlington, Va.: FPLM/John Snow Inc.

Family Planning Logistics Management (1997b), *A Comparative Study on Transportation Models: Directorate of Family Planning Managed Transport and Private Carrier*, Arlington, Va.: FPLM/John Snow Inc.

Family Planning Logistics Management (1998), *Bangladesh CDF: Feasibility Report*, Arlington, Va.: FPLM/John Snow Inc.

Family Planning Logistics Management (2000), *Ghana Cost Study*, Arlington, Va.: FPLM/John Snow Inc.

The Family Planning Manager (1992), 'Improving Contraceptive Supply Management' (September/October), Newton, Mass.: Management Sciences for Health.

The Family Planning Manager (1994), 'Managing Integrated Services' (May/June), Newton, Mass.: Management Sciences for Health.

The Family Planning Manager (1996), 'Focusing on Customer Service' (Spring), Newton, Mass.: Management Sciences for Health.

Felling, Barbara and Walter Proper (1993), 'National Training Strategies in Family Planning Logistics: How Hard Can It Be?', paper presented at the American Public Health Association Meeting, San Francisco, October.

Felling, Barbara and Daniel Thompson (1998), *Training Manual on Training Process Orientation: An FPLM Workshop*, Arlington, Va.: Family Planning Logistics Management/ John Snow Inc.

Fenner, F., D.A. Henderson, I. Arita, Z. Jezek and I.D. Ladnyi (1988), *Smallpox and Its Eradication*, Geneva: World Health Organization.

Forza, Cipriano (1996), 'Achieving Superior Operating Performance from Integrated Pipeline Management: An Empirical Study', *International Journal of Physical Distribution and Logistics Management*, 26: 36–57.

Foster, S.D. (1991), 'Supply and Use of Essential Drugs in Sub-Saharan Africa: Some Issues and Possible Solutions', *Social Science and Medicine*, 32: 1201–18.

Gansler, Jacques S. (1999), 'Public Sector Logistics: Transforming the Way We Do Business', paper presented at the Council of Logistics Management Annual Conference, Toronto, 17–20 October.

Gentry, Connie (1998), 'Logistics IT: Keystone To Integration', *Inbound Logistics* (April): 20–26.

Gentry, Connie (1999), 'Racing the Clock – Small Companies, Big Logistics', *Inbound Logistics* (February): 28–32.

Gilbert, T.F. (1978), *Human Competence: Engineering Worthy Performance*, New York: McGraw-Hill.

Gill, Penny and Jules Abend (1997), 'Wal-Mart: The Supply Chain Heavyweight Champ', *Supply Chain Management Review*, 1 (Spring): 12–20.

Gillis, Chris (1997), 'How Black & Decker Saved $150 Million', *American Shipper* (May): 50–51.

Glisson, Henry T., John W. Handy and Gary S. McCissock (1999), 'Implementing Changes in a Bureaucratic Organization', paper presented at the Council of Logistics Management Annual Conference, Toronto, 17–20 October.

Goddard, Taegan D. and Christopher Riback (1999), 'A Contrary Idea: Don't Run Government Like a Business', *The Washington Post*, 31 January.

Goodwin, Cathy, Stephen J. Grove and Raymond P. Fisk (1996), '"Collaring the Cheshire Cat": Studying Customers' Services Experience through Metaphor', *The Service Industries Journal*, 16 (October): 421–42.

Greenwood, Phil (1997/98), 'Achieving "Customer Delight" Through Logistics', *Competitive Edge* (Winter): 8–7.

Gustin, Craig M. (1993), 'Examination of 10-Year Trends in Logistics Information Systems', *Industrial Engineering* (December): 34–9.

Gustin, Craig M., Patricia J. Daugherty and Theodore P. Stank (1995), 'The Effects of Information Availability on Logistics Integration', *Journal of Business Logistics* 16 (1): 1–21.

Hale, Bernard J. (1999), 'Logistics Perspectives for the New Millennium', *Journal of Business Logistics*, 20 (1): 5–8.

Hammant, Jeremy (1995), 'Information Technology Trends in Logistics', *Logistics Information Management*, 8 (6): 32–38.

Hanson, Kara, Lilian Kumaranayake and Ian Thomas (1998), *Supplying Subsidized Contraceptives: Economic Rationale and Programme Issues for Promoting Sustainability*, prepared for the UK Department for International Development, London: Options Consultancy Services Ltd.

Harrington, Lisa H. (1997), 'Supply Chain Integration from the Inside', *Transportation & Distribution* (March): 35–8.

Harrington, Lisa H. (1998a), 'How to Choose a Third Party Warehouse', *Transportation & Distribution* (November): 112–15.

Harrington, Lisa H. (1998b), 'Software Tools to Revamp your Supply Chain', *Transportation & Distribution* (November): 59–70.

Harrington, Lisa H. (1999a), 'Better Forecasting can Improve your Bottom Line', *Transportation & Distribution* (July): 21–28.

Harrington, Lisa H. (1999b), 'Digital-age Warehousing', *Industry Week* (19 July): 52–8.

Hart, Carolyn (1995), 'State of the Art Logistics', presentation for Logistics Management Training Course, Arlington, Va., September.

Hart, Carolyn (1998a), *Promoting Contraceptive Security: Global Issues in Contraceptive Supply*, draft, Arlington, Va.: FPLM /John Snow Inc.

Hart, Carolyn (1998b), 'Who Cares Enough to Provide Family Planning Supplies?', Talking Points on Global Contraceptive Security, Arlington, Va.

Hart, Carolyn, Kumkum Amin and Steve Hawkins (1999), 'Why is Logistics Important?', presentation for Family Planning Logistics Management, Arlington, Va., May.

Hatry, Harry P., John E. Marcotte, Therese van Houten and Carol H. Weiss (1998), *Customer Surveys for Agency Managers: What Managers Need to Know*, Washington: Urban Institute Press.

Hill, Allan G. (1998), Introductory remarks at the World Bank Conference, 'Adapting to Change: Planning and Delivering Reproductive Health Services within Reforming Health Systems', Nairobi, Kenya, 21–25 September.

Hudock, Brian (1998), 'How to Expand Warehouse Space', *Operations & Fulfillment* (March/April): 16–24.

Hutchings, Jane and Carolyn Hart (1994), 'Contraceptive Commodity Phase-over: A Discussion of Issues Critical to a Shift in Contraceptive Supply Responsibility from USAID to Host Country Programs', draft, Arlington, Va.: FPLM/John Snow Inc.

International Conference on Population and Development (ICPD) (1994), 'Programme of Action', ICPD, Cairo.

Innis, Daniel E. and Bernard J. La Londe (1994), 'Customer Service: The Key to Customer Satisfaction, Customer Loyalty and Market Share', *Journal of Business Logistics*, 15 (1): 1–27.

Jain, Anrudh K. (1989, 'Fertility Reduction and the Quality of Family Planning Services', *Studies in Family Planning*, 20 (1): 1–16.

Keebler, James, Karl B. Manrodt, David A. Durtsche and Michael D. Ledyard (1999), *Keeping Score: Measuring the Business Value of Logistics in the Supply Chain*, Oak Brook, Ill.: Council of Logistics Management.

Kirkpatrick, Donald L. (1996), *Evaluating Training Programs: The Four Levels*, San Francisco: Berrett-Koeher.

Kisubi, Wilson, Francesta Farmer, and Richard Sturgis (1997), *An African Response to the Challenge of Integrating STD/HIV/AIDS Services into Family Planning Programs*, Boston, Mass.: Pathfinder International.

Kols, J.J. and A.J. Sherman (1998), 'Family Planning Programs: Improving Quality', *Population Reports*, Series J, No. 47, Baltimore: Johns Hopkins University School of Public Health, Population Information Program.

Kuglin, Fred A. (1998), *Customer-centered Supply Chain Management: A Link-by-link Guide*, New York: American Management Association.

La Londe, Bernard J. (1996), 'Supply Chain Management: Myth or Reality?', *Supply Chain Management Review* (Summer): 4–5.

La Londe, Bernard J. and Paul H. Zinszer (1976), *Customer Service: Meaning and Measurement*, Chicago, Ill.: National Council of Physical Distribution Management.

Lambert, Douglas M. and James R. Stock (1993), *Strategic Logistics Management*, Homewood, Ill.: Richard D. Irwin Inc.

Lambert, Douglas M. and Thomas C. Harrington (1989), 'Establishing Customer Service Strategies Within the Marketing Mix: More Empirical Evidence', *Journal of Business Logistics*, 10 (2): 44–60.

Lapide, Larry (1998), 'New Developments in Business Forecasting', *The Journal of Business Forecasting* (Spring): 21.

Leenders, Michiel R. and Harold E. Fearon (1997), *Purchasing and Supply Management*, Chicago, Ill.: Richard D. Irwin.

LeMay, Stephen A. and Jon C. Carr (1999), *The Growth and Development of Logistics Personnel*, Oak Brook, Ill.: Council of Logistics Management.

Loudin, Amanda (1997), 'Prescription for Success', *Warehousing Management* (October): 23–6.

Lush, L., J. Cleland, G. Walt and S. Mayhew (1999), 'Integrating Reproductive Health: Myth and Ideology', *Bulletin of the World Health Organization*, 77 (9): 771–7.

Lynch, Clifford F. (1998), 'Leadership in Logistics', *Journal of Business Logistics*, 19 (2): 3–7.

Maggwa, Baker Njugga and Ian Askew (1997), *Integrating STI/HIV Management Strategies into Existing MCH/FP Programs: Lessons from Case Studies in East and Southern Africa*, Nairobi: Africa OR/TA Project II, The Population Council.

Makridakis, Spyros (1986), 'The Art and Science of Forecasting: An Assessment and Future Directions', *International Journal of Forecasting*, 2: 15–39.

Makridakis, Spyros (1990), 'A New Approach to Time Series Forecasting', *Management Science*, 36 (4): 505–51.

'Managing the Supply Chain' (1998), *Global Finance*, 12: 18.

Marien, Ed (1999), 'Quantifying and Benchmarking the Value of the Supply Chain: Metrics, Processes and Benchmarking for Improvement', Madison, Wis.: University of Wisconsin–Madison: School of Business Management Institute.

Mariotti, John L. (1999), 'The Trust Factor in Supply Chain Management', *Supply Chain Management Review* (Spring): 70–77.

Martha, Joseph A. and Robert G. Stevens (1996), 'Tailoring Distribution Channels to Serve Customers Better', *Logistics!* (Fall): 10–15.

Martin, James D. (1997), 'CEOs and Logistics: Thinking out of the Box', *Inbound Logistics*, (June): 22–28.

Mayhew, Susannah (1996), 'Integrating MCH/FP and STD/HIV Services: Current Debates and Future Directions', *Health Policy and Planning*, 11 (4): 339–53.

McGregor, Kieran T. and Yasmin Chandani (2000), 'The Supply Chain in Developing Countries: Strategies for Transformation and Performance Measurement', paper presented at the IPSERA Annual Conference, Toronto.

McKaskill, Tom (1999), 'Inventory Planning: Finding the Right Level', presentation at the Distribution Computer Expo 99, Atlantic City, NJ, 8–9 September.

Melbin, Jodi E. (1996), 'The Changing Face of Logistics Careers', *Distribution* (October): 34–7.

Merrick, Tom (1998), 'Delivering Reproductive Health Services in Health Reform Settings: Challenges and Opportunities', paper, World Bank Conference, 'Adapting to Change: Planning and Delivering Reproductive Health Services within Reforming Health Systems', Nairobi, Kenya, 21–25 September.

Meshcat, Hamid and R.H. Ballou (1996), 'Warehouse Location with Uncertain Stock Availability', *Journal of Business Logistics*, 17 (2): 197–216.

Min, Hokey and William P. Galle (1991), 'International Purchasing Strategies of Multinational US Firms', *International Journal of Purchasing and Materials Management*, 27 (3): 9–18.

Moore, Thomas and Chris Roy (1997), 'Manage Inventory in a Real-time Environment', *Transportation & Distribution* (November): 93–7.

Mottley, Robert (1996), 'Logistics through a Customer's Eyes', *American Shipper* (October): 36.

Muroff, Cindy H. (1997a), 'The Best Supply Chain in the World', *Warehousing Management* (January/February): 47–50.

Muroff, Cindy H. (1997b), 'Warehouses Hold the Cure', *Warehousing Management* (May/June): 20–24.

Murray, Christopher and Alan Lopez (eds) (1996), *The Global Burden of Disease: A Comprehensive Assessment of Mortality and Disability from Diseases, Injuries, and Risk Factors in 1990 and Projected in 2020*, for the World Health Organization and World Bank, Cambridge: Harvard School of Public Health.

Murray, Robert E. and Mary Lou Quinto (1999), 'Enterprise Implementation in a Global Environment', paper presented at Council of Logistics Management Annual Conference, Toronto, 17–20 October.

National Bureau of Statistics (2000), *1999 Tanzania Reproductive and Child Health Survey, Preliminary Report*, Calverton, Md.: Macro International, Inc.

National Council for Population and Development (NCPD) (1995), *Kenya: Family Planning Financial Resource Requirements (1993–2010)*, Republic of Kenya: Office of the Vice President and Ministry of Planning and National Development.

National Council for Population and Development (NCPD), Central Bureau of Statistics (CBS) Ministry of Planning and National Development (Kenya) and Macro International Inc. (1998), *Kenya Demographic and Health Survey*, Calverton, Md.: Macro International Inc.

Ngallaba, Sylvester, Saidi Kapiga, Ireneus Ruyobya and J. Ties Boerma (1993), *Tanzania Demographic and Health Survey (1991/1992)*, Bureau of Statistics and Ministry of Health,

Dar Es Salaam, Tanzania: Bureau of Statistics, Planning Commission; Calverton, Md.: Macro International Inc.

Owens Jr, Richard C. and Timothy Warner (1996), *Concepts of Logistics System Design*, Arlington, Va.: Family Planning Logistics Management/John Snow Inc.

Pagonis, William G. (1992), *Moving Mountains: Lessons in Leadership and Logistics from the Gulf War*, Boston: Harvard Business School Press.

Perry, Steven (1994), *LMIS Assessment Guidelines*, Arlington, Va.: Family Planning Logistics Management/John Snow Inc.

Peters, Eric (1999), 'The Changing Face of Distribution: How Technology Enables Distribution', in *Achieving Supply Chain Excellence through Technology*, 92–95, San Francisco: Montgomery Research Inc.

Pine, B. Joseph II, Don Peppers and Martha Rogers (1995), 'Do You Want To Keep Your Customers Forever?', *Harvard Business Review* (March/April): 103–14.

Ploos van Amstel, M.J. (1990), 'Managing the Pipeline Effectively', *Journal of Business Logistics* 11: 1–25.

Proper, Walter, Carolyn Hart and Abeer Mowaswas (1999), 'Jordan Contraceptives Logistics System: Presentation to Policymakers', paper presented in Amman, Jordan at Family Planning Logistics Management Conference, May.

Quick, Jonathan D. (ed.) (1997), *Managing Drug Supply: The Selection, Procurement, Distribution, and Use of Pharmaceuticals*, West Hartford, Conn.: Kumarian Press.

Quinn, Francis J. (1999), 'Reengineering the Supply Chain: An Interview with Michael Hammer', *Supply Chain Management Review* (Spring): 20–26.

Regional Centre for Quality of Health Care (1999a), 'Distribution Resource Planning (DRP) System', *Better Practices in Reproductive and Child Health: Logistics Support* (BPLS–3), Kampala, Uganda: Institute of Public Health, Makerere University.

Regional Centre for Quality of Health Care (1999b), 'Strengthening STI Logistics Systems to Save Drug Costs and Improve Quality of Care', *Better Practices in Reproductive and Child Health: Logistics Support* (BPLS–1), Kampala, Uganda: Institute of Public Health, Makerere University.

Rhea, Marti J. and David L. Shrock (1987), 'Measuring the Effectiveness of Physical Distribution Customer Service Programs', *Journal of Business Logistics*, 8.

Richardson, Helen L. (1997a), 'People Make Technology Work', *Transportation & Distribution* (February): 39–42.

Richardson, Helen L. (1997b), 'Your CEO Needs to Know', *Transportation & Distribution* (July): 27–31.

Richardson, Helen L. (1998), 'Customer Service Drives Warehouse Choices', *Transportation & Distribution* (December): 59–64.

Ricker, Fred R. and Peter F. Sturtevant (1993), 'Continuous Replenishment Planning (CRP): The Driving Force in the Healthcare Industry', paper presented at the Council of Logistics Management Annual Conference, Washington, DC, 3–6 October.

Robinson, Dana Gaines and James C. Robinson (1998), *Moving from Training to Performance: A Practical Guidebook*, Alexandria, Va.: American Society for Training and Development.

Roush, Chris (1999), *Inside Home Depot*, New York: McGraw Hill.

Ruriani, Deborah Catalano (1996), 'Be a Control Freak', *Warehousing Management* (May/June): 33–5.

Sabath, Robert E. (1996), 'Supply Chain: The Secret Driver of Market Value', *Logistics!*, (Fall): 4–9.

Schary, Philip B. (1992), 'A Concept of Customer Service', *Logistics and Transportation Review*, 28: 341–52.

Schott, Thomas and Robert Degnan (1996), 'What's Your Logistics Department Doing? Inquiring Minds Want to Know', *Distribution* (November): 60–63.

Scott, Charles and Roy Westbrook (1991), 'New Strategic Tools for Supply Chain Management', *International Journal of Physical Distribution and Logistics Management*, 21: 23–33.

Secretan, Lance (1999), 'Inspirational Leadership: Destiny, Calling and Cause', paper presented at the Council of Logistics Management Annual Conference, Toronto, October 17–20.

'Service Industries Mustn't Take Customers for Granted' (1999), *Marketing News* 33 (May 10): 29–31.

Sharma, Arun, Dhruv Grewal and Michael Levy (1995), 'The Customer Satisfaction/Logistics Interface', *Journal of Business Logistics*, 16: 1–21.

Sheffi, Yosef (1990), 'Third Party Logistics: Present and Future Prospects', *Journal of Business Logistics*, 11 (2): 27–39.

Shutt, M., A. Fleuret, S. Kapiga, R. Kirkland, R. Magnani, N. Mandara, G. Mpangile, C. Olson, C. Omari, W. Pressman, S. Ross and J. Safe (1994), *Midterm Review of the Tanzania Family Planning Services Support (FPSS) Project*, Arlington, Va.: POPTECH, Report 94–011–015.

Shycon, Harvey N. (1988, 'Operating Effective "Pipelines"', *Transportation & Distribution*, 29.

Sterling, Jay U. and Douglas M. Lambert (1987), 'Establishing Customer Service Strategies within the Marketing Mix', *Journal of Business Logistics*, 8 (1): 1–30.

Stock, James R. (1990), 'Logistics Thought and Practice: A Perspective', *International Journal of Physical Distribution and Logistics Management*, 20 (1).

Tersine, Richard J. (1994), *Principles of Inventory and Materials Management*, Englewood Cliffs, NJ: PTR Prentice Hall.

United Nations Population Fund (UNFPA) (1993), *Contraceptive Procurement: Options for Program Managers*, New York: UNFPA.

United Nations Population Fund (1994), 'Contraceptive Use and Commodity Costs in Developing Countries 1994–2005', Technical Report No, 18, New York: UNFPA.

United Nations Population Fund (1999a), 'Donor Support for Contraceptives and Logistics 1998', New York: UNFPA.

United Nations Population Fund (1999b), 'The Role of the Logistics Manager in Contraceptive Procurement: A Checklist of Essential Actions', New York: UNFPA.

United Nations Population Fund (n.d.), 'The Global Initiative on Contraceptive Requirements and Logistics Management Needs – Lessons and Methodologies', Technical Report, No. 40, New York: UNFPA.

Waller, Matt, M. Eric Johnson and Tom Davis (1999), 'Vendor–Managed Inventory in the Retail Supply Chain', *Journal of Business Logistics*, 20 (1): 183–203.

Walton, Sam (1992), *Sam Walton: Made in America*, New York: Barton Doubleday Dell Publishing Group.

Warehousing Education and Research Council (WERC) (1997), *A Guide for Establishing Warehouse Job Descriptions*, 2nd edn, Oxford, Ohio: Warehousing Research Center.

Warehousing Education and Research Council (1999), *A Guide to Effective Motivation and Retention Programs in the Warehouse*, Oxford, Ohio: Warehousing Research Center.

The Washington Post (1999), 'A Conversation with Gregory J. Owens', Interview with Manugistics CEO, 1 July.

'What CEOs Should Know About Supply Chain Strategy: An Interview with Robert L. Evans' (1999), *Supply Chain Management Review* (Spring): 27–28.

Wheelwright, Steven C. and Spyros Makridakis (1985), *Forecasting Methods for Management*, New York: John Wiley & Sons.

White, Arlette Campbell (1998), 'The Cairo Programme of Action: A Long Way Still to Go', paper presented at the World Bank Conference, 'Adapting to Change: Planning and Delivering Reproductive Health Services within Reforming Health Systems', Nairobi, Kenya, 21–25 September.

World Bank (1993), *World Development Report 1993: Investing in Health*, New York: Oxford University Press.

Wright, George, Michael J. Lawrence and Fred Collopy (1996), 'The Role and Validity of Judgement in Forecasting', *International Journal of Forecasting*, 12: 1–8.

Zubrod, Justin (1996), 'How Important Is Local Culture to Global Logistics?', *Transportation & Distribution* (December): 61–3.

Index

For Product Safety Concerns and Information please contact our
EU representative GPSR@taylorandfrancis.com Taylor & Francis
Verlag GmbH, Kaufingerstraße 24, 80331 München, Germany